The History of Music Videos

Hal Marcovitz

LUCENT BOOKS
A part of Gale, Cengage Learning

GALE
CENGAGE Learning·

Detroit • New York • San Francisco • New Haven, Conn • Waterville, Maine • London

LIBRARY OF CONGRESS CATALOGING-IN-PUBLICATION DATA

Marcovitz, Hal.
  The history of music videos / by Hal Marcovitz.
       p. cm. -- (The music library)
  Includes bibliographical references and index.
  ISBN 978-1-4205-0821-5 (hardcover : alk. paper)
  1. Music videos--History and criticism--Juvenile literature. I. Title.
  PN1992.8.M87M32 2012
  781.64026'7--dc23   2012004456

Lucent Books
27500 Drake Rd
Farmington Hills MI 48331

ISBN-13: 978-1-4205-0821-5
ISBN-10: 1-4205-0821-0

Printed in the United States of America
1 2 3 4 5 6 7 16 15 14 13 12

CONTENTS

FOREWORD

In the nineteenth century, English novelist Charles Kingsley wrote, "Music speaks straight to our hearts and spirits, to the very core and root of our souls. . . . Music soothes us, stirs us up . . . melts us to tears." As Kingsley stated, music is much more than just a pleasant arrangement of sounds. It is the resonance of emotion, a joyful noise, a human endeavor that can soothe the spirit or excite the soul. Musicians can also imitate the expressive palette of the earth, from the violent fury of a hurricane to the gentle flow of a babbling brook.

The word *music* is derived from the fabled Greek muses, the children of Apollo who ruled the realms of inspiration and imagination. Composers have long called upon the muses for help and insight. Music is not merely the result of emotions and pleasurable sensations, however.

Music is a discipline subject to formal study and analysis. It involves the juxtaposition of creative elements such as rhythm, melody, and harmony with intellectual aspects of composition, theory, and instrumentation. Like painters mixing red, blue, and yellow into thousands of colors, musicians blend these various elements to create classical symphonies, jazz improvisations, country ballads, and rock-and-roll tunes.

Throughout centuries of musical history, individual musical elements have been blended and modified in infinite ways. The resulting sounds may convey a whole range of moods, emotions, reactions, and messages. Music, then, is both an expression and reflection of human experience and emotion.

The foundations of modern musical styles were laid down by the first ancient musicians who used wood, rocks, animal skins—and their own bodies—to re-create the sounds of the natural world in which they lived. With their hands, their feet, and their very breath they ignited the passions of listeners and moved them to their feet. The dancing, in turn, had a mesmerizing and hypnotic effect that allowed people to transcend their worldly concerns. Through music they could achieve a level of shared experience that could not be found in other forms of communication. For this reason, music has always been part of religious endeavors, from ancient Egyptian spiritual ceremonies to modern Christian masses. And it has inspired dance movements from kings and queens spinning the minuet to punk rockers slamming together in a mosh pit.

By examining musical genres ranging from Western classical music to rock and roll, readers will find a new understanding of old music and develop an appreciation for new sounds. Books in Lucent's Music Library focus on the music, the musicians, the instruments, and on music's place in cultural history. The songs and artists examined may be easily found in the CD and sheet music collections of local libraries so that readers may study and enjoy the music covered in the books. Informative sidebars, annotated bibliographies, and complete indexes highlight the text in each volume and provide young readers with many opportunities for further discussion and research.

The Emotional Power of Music Videos

Music videos are capable of drawing emotional responses from fans as well as the performers themselves. Perhaps no music video serves as a better example of this phenomenon than the video produced for pop country star Taylor Swift's hit song "You Belong with Me." The heartfelt story told in the video for Swift's 2009 single illustrates the plight of a teenage girl pining for the football hero who lives next door. She fears he will never love her because he is dating a beautiful cheerleader. As the story unfolds, Swift sheds her wide-rimmed glasses during the senior prom, revealing her beauty. The boy quickly notices, dumps his old girlfriend, and embraces Swift in his arms.

The video features no special effects, camera tricks, overt sexuality, or pyrotechnics that are common in other videos. Still, fans embraced the simple story of love, as well as Swift's obvious talent as a songstress. In fact, in September 2009, the video won the award for Best Female Video at the annual Video Music Awards (VMAs) sponsored by MTV. "Thank you so much!" Swift exclaimed as she was called onto the stage at Radio City Music Hall in New York City to accept the trophy during the nationally broadcast awards show. "I always dreamed about what it would be like to maybe win one of these some day, but I never actually thought it would have happened. I sing country music so thank you so much for giving me a chance to win a VMA award."[1]

Chorus of Boos

Before Taylor Swift could continue her speech, she was interrupted by hip-hop star Kanye West, who bounded onto the stage, grabbing the microphone from the singer's hands. "Yo Taylor, I'm really happy for you," West said. "I'll let you finish, but Beyoncé has one of the best videos of all time. One of the best videos of all time!"[2]

West's declaration and his insistence that pop star Beyoncé should have won for Best Female Video was met by a loud chorus of boos from the audience. As he hopped off the stage, audience members gave Swift a standing ovation. Their support did little to cheer up the mortified country star. Swift hurried away and witnesses later reported seeing the singer crying hysterically backstage.

Taylor Swift's video You Belong with Me *and Kanye West's interruption of her award acceptance speech at the 2009 MTV Video Music Awards illustrate the passion that dominates the art form.*

The drama over the award won by Swift illustrates the passion that dominates the production and performances found in music videos. Since the 1970s and 1980s, music videos have been as much a part of the music business as electric guitars, amplifiers, and drum kits. Says Jeff Ayeroff, president of the recording label Virgin America, "I guess if you ask, 'What changed the music business the most during the Eighties?' It was video."[3]

Since those early days of production, record executives have come to recognize that the quality of a video is as vital to the song's success as the quality of the song itself or the talents of the performer. And video producers have often spared little expense in ensuring that the video—which is often no more than three or four minutes in length—is created by employing the top talent in the music and filmmaking businesses.

Indeed, producers have often spent far more on the production of the video than on the song itself. In 2005 Virgin is believed to have spent $13 million to produce the video for the song "From Yesterday" by the band 30 Seconds to Mars. To produce the video, the band traveled to China, where elaborate sets were constructed and three hundred extras were recruited, each dressed in medieval-style costumes. The video features riders on horseback and eight swordsmen in a brisk duel. The video concludes in a dramatic fireworks display.

Imaginations Run Wild

Other videos approaching that cost were *Scream*, produced for the late Michael Jackson, in which he dances on the ceiling and walls of a mock spaceship at a cost of $7 million, and *Die Another Day* by Madonna, which cost $6 million to produce. The song "Die Another Day" was released as the theme music for a 2002 spy movie of the same name. The video, which helped promote the movie, shows Madonna in the role of a captured spy tortured by the agents of a totalitarian government. Frequent camera cuts show Madonna in a dream sequence, participating in a sword fight with herself.

The videos developed for 30 Seconds to Mars, Jackson, and Madonna show that the creators of music videos often let their imaginations run wild. It would seem that no scenario is too bizarre for use in a music video and, judging by the number of videos in which pop stars are transported into make-believe worlds, it would appear that fans never tire of them, either. On the other hand, when a high-quality yet low-action video such as Taylor Swift's *You Belong with Me* comes along, the artists and the producers also find themselves richly rewarded—even if critics like Kanye West may disagree.

Ironically, West was right: Beyoncé's video for her song "Single Ladies (Put A Ring On It)" was deserving of a Video Music Award. In the video, which was shot in black and white, Beyoncé performs a fast-paced and electrifying dance with two other dancers—their moves choreographed closely in sync. And if West had waited until later in the evening's program, he would have watched Beyoncé win the top award of the night—Video of the Year.

As videos continue to dominate the music business, chances are there will be similar controversies in the future. Swift, Beyoncé, and West are sure to appear again on the stage of the Video Music Awards—if not as winners, then certainly as representatives of an art that is limited only by the talents and imaginations of its performers and producers.

CHAPTER 1

The Roots of Music on Video

O n October 6, 1927, movie audiences sat enthralled as they saw—and heard—something very new. That was the day the film *The Jazz Singer* debuted in American theaters. Until then, movies had always been silent—no dialogue was spoken, because engineers had not yet found a way to synchronize sound to film. Instead, the very limited dialogue included in the films was printed on cards that were photographed and inserted into the action on screen. Films frequently featured musical accompaniment, but that was typically accomplished by a piano or organ player hired by the theater owner.

The movie industry suddenly changed when *The Jazz Singer* premiered in theaters. Starring singer Al Jolson, the film falls short of being a full "talkie"—much of the action is still carried on in silence—but snatches of dialogue are spoken by the actors, and all of the songs are performed by Jolson. In fact, Jolson sings the first of the movie's songs just a few minutes into the film. That song was "Toot, Toot, Tootsie," a popular and lighthearted dance number of the era. "The movie was a tremendous hit," says historian Nathan Miller. "*The Jazz Singer* was the top-grossing film of the year although only five hundred theaters in the whole country were wired for sound."[4]

It could be argued that every artist performing in a music

video produced today—from Rihanna shimmying through *Only Girl (In the World)* to Justin Timberlake letting his heart bleed in *Cry Me A River*—owes something to Jolson's performance of "Toot, Toot, Tootsie." Certainly, Jolson's rendition includes none of the stagecraft found in the typical video of the twenty-first century: The steadfast camera focuses on Jolson and does not move as he performs the song while standing in front of an orchestra—although he does occasionally break into some very limited dancing. Still, Jolson's song was the first piece of music to emerge

The Jazz Singer was the first movie to contain sound, including Al Jolson (pictured) singing.

Music and Magic Lanterns

The idea of pairing music to pictures goes back as far as 1863, through the use of a device known as the magic lantern. These machines were similar to the slide projectors that were popular during the 1950s and 1960s. A songwriter, Tony Pastor, obtained lantern slide portraits of Civil War generals and projected them onto screens before audiences as singers performed his song "Heroes of the War."

In 1894, a magic lantern presentation of the song "The Little Lost Child" was a hit on the New York stages that were known as vaudeville theater. Photographer George H. Thomas projected his touching images of children onto a screen while singer Allen May performed the song. Says film historian Rick Altman, "By the end of the [nineteenth] century, illustrated songs were a vaudeville fixture. In this early period, sixteen to twenty slides would be used to illustrate each song. Photographed in black and white with live models staged to represent the words to the song, the slides would then be hand-colored and projected while a singer belted out the lyrics. Audiences would usually be invited to join in the chorus, reading the words off the screen."

Rick Altman. *Silent Film Sound.* New York: Columbia University Press, 2004, p. 107.

from the mouth of a singer on film—a technical achievement that makes today's music videos possible. In fact, just before launching into the song, Jolson provides a highly prescient comment about what the future holds when he announces: "You ain't heard nothin' yet!"[5]

Madonna Channels Marilyn Monroe

As Hollywood moved into the 1930s and 1940s, it was clear to the producers of the era that movie audiences loved musicals. Typically, these films featured boy-meets-girl sce-

narios, but the thin plots were invariably interrupted as the stars broke into song and dance. Moreover, the musical sequences always seemed to provide stories within themselves—it didn't much matter to the audience that when Fred Astaire, a major musical star of the era, tap-danced to the song "Puttin' on the Ritz" in the 1946 film *Blue Skies*, the four-minute scene actually had very little to do with the plot of the movie. But the audience members sure enjoyed the visual specter of the world's best tap dancer going through his steps as nine versions of himself—a feat of trick photography—matched him step for step in the background. Years later, such playful photo effects would become a staple of modern music video production.

Otherwise, a clear example of how the musicals of the era later inspired music video producers can be found in the song-and-dance segment of the 1953 film *Gentlemen Prefer Blondes*, in which starlet Marilyn Monroe is showered with jewels by tuxedoed dancers while she performs the song "Diamonds Are a Girl's Best Friend." Three decades later, Madonna's video for her hit song "Material Girl" provided a much similar scenario. In fact, according to Madonna, the plot for her 1985 video was directly inspired by the scene from the 1953 film. "Well, my favorite scene in all of Monroe's movies is when she does that dance sequence for 'Diamonds Are a Girl's Best Friend,'" Madonna said. "And when it came time to do the video for ['Material Girl'], I said, 'I can just redo that whole scene and it'll be perfect.'"[6]

The popularity of movie musicals like *Gentlemen Prefer Blondes* prompted the studios to produce short musical films, most no more than a few minutes in length, to be shown before the main features. Years ago it was not unusual for theaters to provide several "short subjects" to be shown to audiences prior to the main attraction; these features might have included animated cartoons, brief documentaries, newsreels showing visual images and narration of stories in the news, and brief comedy or musical features. Among the singers and musicians featured in the musical shorts were jazz singer Billie Holiday, crooner Bing Crosby, and jazz pianist and conductor Duke Ellington. Typically, these stars performed their hits onstage with a minimum of dancing, special effects, or other features found in modern music videos. Still, they were films made specifically to showcase music.

Animation Linked to Music Videos

As movie audiences enjoyed musicals on screen, animation was coming into its own as a form of popular entertainment during this era—and it didn't take long for music to become a component of the images audiences saw on the screen. In Germany in 1925, animator Oscar Fischinger, artist Matthias Holl, and Hungarian composer Alexander László collaborated on a series of short cartoons that synchronized images with music. These were highly abstract works: Holl produced geometric shapes rendered in watercolors that Fischinger transferred to film, then set to László's music. These brief films certainly do not portray singers mouthing lyrics; nevertheless, Holl's brightly colored squares and circles move rhythmically across the screen in time to the beat of László's music.

A year after *The Jazz Singer* debuted in theaters, animators Walt Disney and Ub Iwerks produced a brief cartoon titled *Steamboat Willie* that played in theaters as a short subject. *Steamboat Willie* stars Mickey Mouse and Minnie Mouse, introducing two characters who remain enormously popular more than eight decades after their images first appeared on movie screens. Like in *The Jazz Singer*, the action in *Steamboat Willie* is synchronized with sound, and the sounds the audience hears are mostly musical. (Minnie plays a version of the American folk song "Turkey in the Straw" by cranking the tail of a goat.)

Disney would go on to found one of the most successful entertainment companies in America. Today the Walt Disney Company owns film studios, TV networks, theme parks, and other businesses, but animation has always been an important part of the company's success. And thanks to Disney, animated cartoons have become more sophisticated, featuring dialogue as well as music, dancing, and singing by the animated characters—often voiced by major Hollywood stars.

In 1940 the Disney studio produced the feature-length film *Fantasia*. Essentially a film composed of a string of unrelated stories set to classical music, *Fantasia* would serve as an inspiration for the music video producers to come. It features a lot of off-the-wall ideas—specifically a performance of the ballet "Dance of the Hours" in which ballerinas portrayed by tutu-wearing hippos are twirled through the air by runty crocodiles. Many of the scenes featured in *Fantasia* are the work of Oscar Fischinger, who by this time had moved to the United States

In 1940 Walt Disney produced the full-length feature film Fantasia, *which would go on to influence music videos decades later.*

and gone to work for Disney. According to music critic Jim Farber and film critic Glenn Kenny, collaborators on a history of music videos for *Rolling Stone* magazine, there is a direct link that connects the early animations of the 1920s, the production of *Fantasia*, and modern music videos. According to Farber and Kenny,

> Going back to the birth of film, there was a synergy between sound and image (the piano music employed to accompany silent films). But Oscar Fischinger in the '20s was the first person to reverse the process by making his images conform to the sound. Such an arrangement gave Fischinger great leeway for creating whatever visuals the music suggested, often taking the form of abstract geometric shapes. Even more creative were the whimsical images Fischinger (and scores of other artists) contributed to Walt Disney's *Fantasia* in 1940, which ultimately made it the first unintentional long-form music video.[7]

Music Arrives on TV

Theaters weren't the only places people could watch singing and dancing on film. By the 1940s, so-called Soundie machines were finding their way into diners, taverns, and nightclubs. The Soundie machine was a variation of the jukebox. For ten cents a customer could not only play a favorite song, but see a brief film produced to accompany the song on the Soundie screen. As such, another step toward the musical video had been taken: To help sell a record, the performer was expected to appear in the Soundie film as well. Soundies frequently showed the singers performing their songs onstage, or in a nightclub setting, but they also frequently featured leggy dancers wearing skimpy costumes—much as videos typically do today.

Another development that occurred during the 1940s that would prove important to the future of music videos was the growth of television. By the end of 1946, about 10,000 television sets could be found in American homes as well as other places—mostly taverns. By the end of 1949, there were 2 million TV sets in America. Ten years later, Americans owned 42 million TV sets.

As television grew into an important source of entertainment, executives at TV networks scrambled to find programming to fill long hours of airtime. To fill in the gaps between the early dramas, situation comedies, and variety shows of the 1940s and 1950s, TV producers filmed brief musical performances that could be inserted at the bottom of the hour to fill in the two or three minutes before the next program was scheduled to air. As with the Soundie films, these vignettes typically featured singers or musicians performing their songs onstage. Nevertheless, as TV networks aired these features, they made them available to wider audiences than was possible through the Soundie machines.

Rock and Roll Arrives on Film

Back in the diners and taverns, video jukeboxes had taken a step beyond the Soundie machines with the introduction of the Scopitone machines. Like the Soundies, the Scopitone films featured musical stars of the era performing their

Soundies and Scopitones

Soundie films could be viewed on a small but complicated machine known as the Panoram, which displayed brief films viewed on a small screen. Panorams were installed mostly in taverns and diners. Generally, eight Soundie films were spliced together in a loop and each musical performance could be viewed for a dime. A company known as RCM Productions produced many of the Soundie films of the 1940s. A founder of the company was James Roosevelt, the son of President Franklin D. Roosevelt.

The Scopitone machine represented an advancement over the Panoram. The refrigerator-sized machine was developed in France in the years following World War II by engineers who used surplus military parts. On a conventional jukebox, a listener could drop in a coin and select from a list of dozens of songs. The developers of the Scopitone operated under the same concept: Instead of being forced to watch whatever was spliced together inside the Panoram machine, the viewer had a choice of several films to watch that were looped inside the Scopitone. By the mid-1960s, some five hundred Scopitone machines had been installed in diners, taverns, and similar public venues.

hits, but the producers of these films managed to tell stories in these brief films: They often featured young couples encountering one another at parties or other social events, dancing, frolicking, and getting romantic.

Scopitone films could also step outside the norm, providing the type of scenarios music video producers would later embrace. In 1966 singer Joi Lansing made a Scopitone film to promote her single "Trapped in a Web of Love." The scenario for the short film shows the singer entangled in a huge spider web while she pines for her lost lover.

The songs and scenarios featured in Soundies and Scopitones may have been the forerunners of today's music videos, but they were not aimed at youthful audiences—their

audiences were more likely made up of mothers and fathers. By then, though, the movies had discovered rock-and-roll music. Elvis Presley was a big star. So were Frankie Avalon and Annette Funicello, Bobby Rydell, Fabian, and Ann-Margret. Their movies feature singing and dancing and, as with the movie musicals of the 1930s and 1940s, it didn't matter to the young fans in the audience that the musical scenes didn't seem to have much to do with the plot of the film. Anybody today who can find the 1957 Presley film *Jailhouse Rock* on DVD or broadcast on a nostalgia movie network will see Presley and dancers performing the title track wearing striped costumes, swinging on cell doors, dancing on mess hall tables, and generally having a good time in prison. Even the guards rock. It is a lighthearted moment in a film that otherwise tells the dour story of an inmate (played by Presley) jailed for killing a man in a bar

By the 1950s, movies had discovered rock and roll. Elvis Presley (dancing, front) made several of these types of movies, including Jailhouse Rock.

fight. Moreover, video jukeboxes would continue to live on into the 1970s; the electronics company Rock America produced a more sophisticated version of the Soundie and Scopitone machines, installing them in bars and nightclubs.

Beatles and Monkees

In a forerunner to the music video, the Beatles film A Hard Day's Night *made use of innovative camera work set to their music.*

Two developments in the 1960s would provide major steps toward the birth of the music video. First, the Beatles emerged as international rock-and-roll stars. Hoping to capitalize on the popularity of the British rockers, Hollywood produced a 1964 film featuring the group titled *A Hard Day's Night*. Directed by British filmmaker Richard Lester, the movie offered the thinnest of plots—essentially, a madcap day in the life of the mop-topped lads as they prepare

for a concert. The real attraction of the film is the performance of the group's hit songs, which were largely filmed as miniature stories in themselves. For example, the song "Can't Buy Me Love" is performed as the Beatles are photographed through the use of swooping overhead crane shots while the band members horse around in an open field. Says music critic Saul Austerlitz,

> As with so many other things, the Beatles were innovators in the music video format. Intended as a quick cash-in on their overnight success, the Beatles' first film, *A Hard Day's Night*, directed by Richard Lester, was an accidental comic classic and a key precursor to the music video. Beatles songs provide a wall-to-wall sonic carpet for the film, and Lester artfully moves the music background to foreground and back again. Lester turns the musical numbers into discrete short films, less about the stately strumming of guitars than dazzling, unhinged expressions of male camaraderie, clever hijinks and . . . physical humor.[8]

Eager to capitalize on the success of *A Hard Day's Night*, Hollywood executives quickly rushed other movies starring rock-and-roll stars into production. Among the films that made it to theater screens during this era were *Having a Wild Weekend* in 1965, starring the Dave Clark Five; *Love & Kisses* in 1965 with teen idol Ricky Nelson; *Finders Keepers* in 1966 with Cliff Richard and his band, the Shadows; and *Mrs. Brown You've Got a Lovely Daughter* in 1968, starring Peter Noone and his band, Herman's Hermits. Each movie features a thin plot—a circumstance that the teenage audiences seemed willing to overlook as long as the action paused from time to time so that the bands could play their hit songs.

The other major development of the 1960s was the premiere of the TV show *The Monkees*. Composed of four musicians cast to play members of a rock-and-roll band, the show featured silly plots, but each week the band performed a song. As with *A Hard Day's Night* and other rock-and-roll movies of the era, the scenarios for the songs often had little to do with the plot of the week's episode. "Almost inevitably, there would be a montage set to one of their songs, in which

Who Were the Monkees?

Most rock bands are born in somebody's garage or basement, where musically talented friends meet to develop their sound. If they are talented and lucky, they may find stardom. As for the Monkees, they started out on top.

Anxious to cash in on the popularity of rock-and-roll music in the 1960s, TV executives Bob Rafelson and Bert Schneider developed a situation comedy featuring the comic antics of a rock-and-roll band they named the Monkees. They put out a casting call for musician-actors, and after auditioning dozens of candidates, selected their four band members: singer Davy Jones, a British actor who had appeared in theatrical musicals; drummer Micky Dolenz, son of well-known dramatic actor George Dolenz; guitarist Mike Nesmith, who had been performing in Los Angeles, California, folk music clubs; and bass guitarist Peter Tork, who was working as a dishwasher when he heard about the Monkees casting call.

Jones, Dolenz, Nesmith, and Tork scored several hits during their three years on network TV, including "Daydream Believer," "Last Train to Clarksville," and "I'm a Believer." Over the years, members of the Monkees have occasionally reunited for concerts and tours. Jones passed away in 2012.

the band horsed around on the beach, rode dune buggies, or battled baddies," says Austerlitz. "These interludes are music videos of a sort, rarely advancing the plot in any significant way."[9]

The Monkees lasted three seasons, finally going off the air in 1968. Still, one of the members of the band, Mike Nesmith, took the lessons he learned from the show and the production of its music to heart. In the years to come, he would serve as one of the first producers of what today would be categorized as music videos.

From *Midnight Special* to MTV

Fans of *The Monkees* may have been entertained by the band's music, but the producers intended the show to be a comedy. Otherwise, there were just a handful of serious rock-music-oriented shows on TV at the time. Moreover, these shows lacked wide audiences because they were not generally aired in "prime time"—the evening hours of 8 p.m. to 11 p.m., when most people are expected to be watching TV. For example, *Midnight Special*, which debuted in 1973, was broadcast on NBC; it featured both live and taped performances from some of the top rock stars of the era, but it was aired from 12:30 a.m. to 2 a.m. on Saturday mornings. Among the other shows of the era that featured rock music were *Soundstage from Chicago*, which was telecast by PBS; the British-produced *Kenny Everett Video Show*, which was syndicated to local TV stations in the United States; and another syndicated program, *Don Kirshner's Rock Concert*.

In 1975 *Midnight Special* featured what is believed to have been the first music video produced specifically for a recorded single—the ballad "Bohemian Rhapsody" by the British group Queen. The six-minute video includes mostly studio footage of the band members, but there are some special effects added—mostly fade-in and fade-out camera shots, double exposures, shadowy images of the band members, and some trick photography in which the four musicians' images are multiplied as though they are being viewed through a prism. The *Bohemian Rhapsody* video was produced specifically to promote the band's album *A Night at the Opera*, which features the single. It took four hours to film the video; production costs were a mere $7,000. *Midnight Special* replayed the video several times in 1975 and 1976, helping the song remain on *Billboard* magazine's Hot 100 Singles chart for twenty-four weeks.

Other bands saw the effect the *Bohemian Rhapsody* video was having on the sales of the album and rushed to make their own videos. In 1976 the metal band AC/DC produced a video for the song "Jailbreak." Glam rocker David Bowie also embraced the concept and produced a number of videos for his songs.

In 1978 Mike Nesmith produced a solo album, *From a*

Radio Engine to a Photon Wing, which features the single "Rio." To help promote the album, Nesmith filmed a video for "Rio." The video depicts Nesmith singing the song accompanied by three backup singers, as their images are projected over ocean waves as well as a background of stars and planets. Even by 1970s standards, the special effects were very weak. Nevertheless, the album turned out to be a big hit in Great Britain and several other European nations thanks to the willingness of music-oriented TV shows in those countries to feature the video for "Rio." In America, though, the video for "Rio" received little airtime, undoubtedly contributing to the lackluster acceptance for Nesmith's album in the United States. Indeed, the album never cracked *Billboard* magazine's Top 200 list.

Despite the tepid acceptance for his music videos in America, Nesmith still had faith in the future of music produced as a visual medium. Even as *From a Radio Engine to a Photon Wing* stumbled along at the bottom of the American charts, Nesmith said, "I thought, 'My gosh, the potential for this artistically is staggering.' I just really want to get into it."[10]

In 1981 Nesmith used his family's fortune (his mother had invented Liquid Paper, a fluid that corrects typewritten errors, a very important product in the pre-computer era) to produce a TV pilot titled *Elephant Parts*. It was a sixty-minute variety show, featuring comedy and music, but the music was presented in a video format. In fact, the pilot featured five videos. Nesmith was unable to sell the pilot to a network; instead, it was released directly on videocassette, where it chalked up healthy sales. By now, American TV producers had warmed to the notion of featuring music videos in their broadcasts. Portions of *Elephant Parts* were played on such shows as *Saturday Night Live* and *Don Kirshner's Rock Concert*—which helped promote the tape and enhance its sales. Moreover, *Elephant Parts* would go on to make music history when it won the first Grammy Award for a music video in 1981.

Other artists were also experimenting with video. As videos from *Elephant Parts* were finding playtime on music-oriented TV shows, a number of other videos were produced, featuring such performers as Blondie, Elton John, ABBA, Loretta Lynn, Olivia Newton-John, Fleetwood Mac, and ex-Beatle Paul McCartney, who was now heading the band Wings.

In the meantime, Nesmith produced a new series, a thirty-minute show of music videos titled *PopClips*. He sold the series to the youth-oriented network Nickelodeon, owned by the huge media company Time Warner. In 1981 *PopClips* ran weekly on Nickelodeon, but did not survive for a second season. Instead, Time Warner's entertainment division, Warner Communications, had much bigger plans. Encouraged by the success of *PopClips*, as well as the trend among performers to produce music videos, executives at Warner Communications hatched plans to launch a twenty-four-hour cable network devoted entirely to music videos. The name of the network said it all: Music Television—or MTV, for short.

CHAPTER 2

"I Want My MTV"

MTV made its debut on August 1, 1981. The first words uttered on the new cable TV station were, "Ladies and gentleman, rock 'n' roll."[11] They were spoken by John Lack, one of the creators of the new channel, as viewers watched a brief film of a rocket blasting off from a launchpad. Seconds later, the first video aired on MTV: *Video Killed the Radio Star* by the British new-wave group the Buggles. The song and video tell the story of the golden age of radio, and how recording artists would fail to find TV an effective medium to display their art. The video features the band performing the song amid a strange jungle of TV sets as well as old-fashioned radios and jukeboxes while a confused little girl wanders through the mess.

For MTV executives, the choice of the premiere video was, of course, an inside joke. The producers of the new cable channel certainly did expect TV to be a very effective medium for the performance of music. In any event, it isn't likely that many people saw this history-making performance by the Buggles. For starters, MTV aired its premiere video at 12:01 a.m. Also, the channel was not yet available nationwide. In fact, on the day of its premiere, the only portion of the country where MTV was available was a part of New Jersey.

Still, music videos now had their own twenty-four-hour

cable channel—the best showcase ever for this new form of entertainment. No longer would fans have to pour coins into a Rock America machine or wait for the occasional video to be played on a TV variety show. MTV intended to play videos twenty-four hours a day, seven days a week. On its first day on the air, MTV featured videos by such major rock stars of the era as Pat Benatar, Rod Stewart, the Pretenders, REO Speedwagon, Fleetwood Mac, Blondie, the Who, and Todd Rundgren.

MTV represents a driving force in the early development of music videos, proving the existence of a huge and hungry audience for music video entertainment. MTV's groundbreaking work in displaying both the vocal and visual talents of rock-and-roll stars revolutionized the industry—making the production of the video just as important as the production of the song.

MTV served another purpose: It helped rock performers build their careers, and also helped make big stars even bigger. "You'd be walking down the street, and somebody would say, 'Hey man, I saw you on MTV,'" says George Thorogood, singer and guitarist for George Thorogood and the Delaware Destroyers. "That was very groovy. It wasn't, 'I saw you on TV.' It was, 'I saw you on MTV.'"[12]

The Veejays

The music videos provided the programming, but MTV executives wanted the channel to be more than just music videos strung together without breaks—as though they were looped through a Soundie machine. On the radio, disc jockeys, or DJs, introduce the songs and add their own commentary and personalities to their shows. MTV wanted the same format for its broadcasts, and therefore opted to feature "veejays"—young people who would appear on camera, talking about the performers, the music, and the videos and adding their own personalities to the broadcasts. Alan Hunter, one of MTV's first veejays, recalled the day of the network's launch:

When it came to the actual launch, we all got into a bus in Manhattan—because they didn't have [the MTV channel] in Manhattan—and had to go out to a little restaurant-bar in New Jersey to watch the actual kick-off. So we got in the bus, we got totted out there, and there were hundreds of MTV employees and family members. My heart racing a mile a minute. . . .

So after the Buggles came on, we all just looked at each other and said . . . "This might just get big . . . if we can last." Of course, the next day, we all had to get to work.[13]

MTV featured regular veejays who hosted their own programs. Each week, a dozen or more guest veejays would be invited to appear as well—usually celebrities who regarded MTV as a vehicle to boost their careers. Among the guest veejays to appear on MTV during the 1980s were model Cindy Crawford, basketball star Shaquille O'Neal, and pro hockey player Adam Oates.

The first MTV veejays—(clockwise from top) Mark Goodman, J.J. Jackson, Martha Quinn, Alan Hunter, and Nina Blackwood—added their own unique personalities to the broadcasts.

Each of the regular veejays soon developed their own styles as well as their own followings of loyal fans. Martha Quinn's "girl next door" looks helped her connect with the young fans. Hunter acted like the resident class clown, specializing in foreign accents, gags, and physical humor. "You break stuff and you don't read the script," Hunter says. "That's the key. That was really kind of MTV's whole thing."[14]

Nina Blackwood and her wild mop of blond hair represented the free spirit among the veejays. Mark Goodman presented himself as a serious student of popular music. J.J. Jackson brought a broadcast journalism background to MTV and could often persuade major stars of the era to appear on his show for interviews. Among the rock stars who sat down for interviews with Jackson were Pete Townshend of the Who and Robert Plant of Led Zeppelin. The network also featured news reporters Kurt Loder and Tabitha Soren, providing fans with updates on news in the world of popular music.

It didn't take long for the veejays to become as popular as the rock bands whose videos they were introducing. Blackwood recalls making a promotional visit to San Antonio, Texas, and finding crowds of young people waiting to meet her. Says Blackwood, "The limo is taking me to an autograph signing session at a record store. We're going into this shopping center, and I see this line wrapped all around. I'm going, 'Oh, wow, who's here?' And my [guide] says, 'Well . . . *you*.' I go, 'WHAT?!' There were hundreds of people there."[15]

The Popularity of Narrowcasting

It may have been a vibrant and exciting time for the founders and veejays of MTV, but it had taken some thirty years of technological advancement, as well as government approval, before the cable channel could deliver its first videos to its young audience. Cable TV was first developed in the late 1940s as a method of delivering TV signals to rural homes too remote to pick up the over-the-air broadcasts of the major networks. Huge antennas were erected atop mountains in places like rural Arkansas, Oregon, and Pennsylvania, and were connected to nearby homes by buried cables. Otherwise, city and suburban residents received signals by erecting antennas on their roofs or

Not "MTV Friendly"

MTV may have helped performers like Madonna and Michael Jackson reach wide audiences and become major recording stars, but it could be argued that the network—and the whole industry of music video production—helped cut short the careers of many talented pop stars. The reason: Many of these performers lacked sex appeal.

The singer Christopher Cross serves as a prime example. In 1979 he released his debut album, *Christopher Cross*, which went on to win five Grammy Awards. But Cross was husky and balding and, as a result, his videos received scant play on MTV and elsewhere. "It wasn't even about the music anymore," says singer Frank Stallone. "Christopher Cross came out with one of the best break-out solo albums I'd ever heard. But then all of a sudden when they saw him—and he looked like this truck driver—it killed him. I saw him [on stage]. This guy had a beautiful voice, and you're figuring this really cool-looking guy will come out . . . and he came out looking like Bluto [the villain from the Popeye cartoons]. I felt really bad for him because he was really good. So he was definitely not 'MTV friendly.'"

Quoted in Greg Prato. *MTV Ruled the World: The Early Years of Music Video*. London: Lulu, 2010, pp. 67–68.

extending the "rabbit ear" aerials found atop the TV sets of the era.

The idea that cable TV could carry its own programming surfaced in the 1960s when cable operators first floated the idea of offering unique programming to their subscribers, but these plans were stymied by the major television networks—NBC, CBS, and ABC—which wanted to control all of the TV programming. The networks exerted pressure on the US Federal Communications Commission (FCC), which regulates TV transmissions, to bar upstart cable companies from carrying original programming. Finally, though, in 1972, the FCC eased the restrictions, clearing the way for cable companies to create their own programming. The first to do so was Home Box Office, now known as HBO, which offered movies and other original programs to subscribers for a monthly fee. Another early entrant in the cable movement was the Atlanta, Georgia, TV station WTBS, owned by billionaire Ted Turner. Turner saw the potential of cable, and offered his TV station to nationwide cable systems. By the end of the 1970s, some 16 million homes were wired for cable.

As cable systems grew, entrepreneurs discovered the popularity of what became known as narrowcasting—designing programming for specific demographics of viewers. As such, the cable network Nickelodeon was launched for very young viewers. American Movie Classics features programming for fans of vintage films. Cable News Network, now known as CNN, offers news twenty-four hours a day, while ESPN provides sports programming round-the-clock. C-SPAN placed cameras in the chambers of the US House and Senate so that Americans could watch their government's leaders at work. And as ex-Monkee Mike Nesmith was showing the potential of music videos through his *PopClips* and *Elephant Parts* programs, executives at Warner Communications envisioned a channel narrowcast to an audience of young people eager to see music videos on their TV screens.

Thriller Breaks the Record

As it turned out, that audience would exceed all expectations. By the end of its first year, MTV had grown beyond its tiny New Jersey base and was now available nationwide. After just twelve months on the air, MTV was being viewed by 2.1 million subscribers. By the end of the network's second year on cable, the audience had grown to nearly 10 million. And by the end of its first decade, MTV was reaching some 50 million American homes. The network's slogan, "I Want My MTV," certainly spoke volumes about the cable network most teenagers preferred to watch. Moreover, the network was adding programming other than just music videos. It produced news shows, such as *The Day in Rock* and *The Week in Rock*, providing news and commentary about the music scene.

With MTV's audiences now totaling in the millions, it didn't take long for many of the major pop artists to produce

MTV's Color Barrier

Michael Jackson's videos helped break what had become a color barrier at MTV. Before the videos for "Thriller," "Beat It," and "Billie Jean" were produced, MTV featured few videos starring black artists. The network's research department had determined that its primary demographic was white suburban teenagers who were not fans of black urban music. In fact, of the 750 videos shown on MTV during the network's first eighteen months, fewer than 24 featured black artists. Ironically, many of the white artists featured on MTV performed songs that had originally been recorded by black singers. "When videos of black artists were submitted, they were quickly rejected as not being 'rock 'n' roll," says a Jackson biographer, J. Randy Taraborrelli.

MTV at first rejected *Billie Jean*, but agreed to air the video after the video's producer, CBS Records, threatened to withdraw all its videos from MTV. *Billie Jean* made its debut on MTV in March 1983 in "heavy rotation," meaning it was aired frequently. *Billie Jean* was quickly followed on the air by *Beat It* and *Thriller*.

J. Randy Taraborrelli. *Michael Jackson: The Magic, the Madness, the Whole Story.* New York: Grand Central, 2010, p. 252.

videos specifically so MTV could showcase their music. The videos produced for these performers set increasingly high standards for camera work, choreography, and production value. In just a handful of years, the art of music video production had come a long way since the days when images of Mike Nesmith and his backup singers were superimposed over ocean waves, or the members of Queen were photographed through a prism.

During the 1980s, the late Michael Jackson—a truly incandescent performer—starred in a series of music videos that set the gold standard for video production. These videos were produced for his songs "Beat It," "Billie Jean," and "Thriller." Released in 1983, "Billie Jean" tells the story of a young man denying that he has fathered an illegitimate son.

Michael Jackson's Thriller *video was so popular that MTV ran it twice an hour after its release in 1983.*

"A video for 'Billie Jean' was made for the then relatively new music television channel MTV," says a Jackson biographer, Lisa D. Campbell. "Michael dances his way to Billie Jean's hotel room, with each segment of the sidewalk lighting up at his touch. It is here that Michael shows how his dancing abilities have advanced. He performs lightning quick spins and then freeze frames poised up on his toes. Arriving at the hotel, he climbs the staircase to her room, each stair lighting up as he steps, even the burned out 'HOTEL' sign lights up letter by letter as he passes."[16]

Beat It would also illustrate how video could be an ideal medium to showcase Jackson's skills as a singer and dancer while also adding a strong dose of drama and high-quality production standards. Also airing on MTV in 1983, *Beat It* dramatizes Jackson's efforts to stop a gang rumble. "At the start of the video, the members of two rival gangs emerge from the streets, pool halls, and even the sewers to face each other in an empty warehouse," says Campbell. "Michael shows up just in time to prevent possible bloodshed. Instead of battling, Michael convinces the opposing forces to join him in dance. 'Beat It' features some of the best moves ever, and has become a classic video."[17]

But it was the video for "Thriller" that would become a national phenomenon—it was so popular that soon after its release in December 1983, MTV ran it twice an hour. *Thriller* was far different than any other video that had yet been produced. For starters, it ran fourteen minutes long—most videos typically span no more than three or four minutes. It cost $600,000 to produce—at the time, the average cost for producing a music video was $25,000. And it was directed by John Landis, a Hollywood film director. Jackson had recently seen Landis's horror movie *An American Werewolf in London* and appealed to Landis to direct the video version of "Thriller."

The video is, indeed, a horror story. While on a date with his girlfriend, Jackson turns into a "werecat." He is soon joined by a cadre of ghouls, whom he leads in a tightly choreographed dance that would soon become a staple of virtually every American high school prom. Says Landis, "What 'Thriller' did, and not by design, was totally prove the viability of the rock video as a selling tool, and establish Michael Jackson as a demigod."[18] In fact, before the video was released, the album containing "Thriller" (also named *Thriller*) sold 25 million copies. After the video was released, sales of *Thriller* shot up to 45 million. Eventually, sales of the album *Thriller* would go over the 100 million mark, making it the top-selling album of all time.

Madonna Pushes the Limits

Michael Jackson was not the only superstar who owed a large measure of success to MTV and this new medium of music video. During the 1980s and beyond, Jackson's main rival in pop music was Madonna, who would certainly use the music video to showcase her talents and help sell her music.

In 1989 Madonna's video for her single "Express Yourself" featured her as a factory boss, prancing about as the head of a workforce of hunky, shirtless male workers. The dark and moody sets were intricately designed, based on the sets used in *Metropolis*, a 1927 silent film about the seamy underbelly of a totalitarian society. "Since her career began at roughly the same time as the behemoth network, Madonna and MTV are forever intertwined," says *Rolling Stone* music critic Jancee Dunn. "As our girl morphed [into] the world's most famous woman, so, too, did MTV evolve into a sleek superpower. No video is sleeker or more superpowered than 'Express Yourself.'"[19]

Madonna soon followed up *Express Yourself* with the equally sexy *Vogue* and *Justify My Love*, both in 1990. "Vogue" is a fast-paced dance song; its video is filmed in black and white. In some of the scenes, Madonna wears a top that is nearly see-through. And in *Justify My*

Madonna continued to push the limits of what was acceptable in music videos with Erotica *in 1992.*

Love, Madonna and her dancers shed most of their clothes in some highly charged, sexually suggestive scenes.

By now, Madonna and such other stars of the era as Samantha Fox, Kylie Minogue, and Shakira were clearly basing the scenarios of their videos on their personal sex appeal and knockout looks, pushing the limits of what could be shown on the public airwaves. As far as MTV was concerned, though, with *Justify My Love* Madonna had taken it a step too far. The network refused to air the video.

MTV Under Attack

Still, there was no question that sex was becoming a big part of MTV's programming. Many music videos told romantic stories and often featured nearly nude performers in passionate embraces, although quick camera cuts broke away from the action before things got too revealing. And yet what was a parent to think when he or she walked into the family room, finding the television tuned to MTV while the network aired the 1984 Van Halen video *Hot for Teacher*, in which a sexy middle school teacher stripteases for her students? Or the J. Geils Band's 1981 hit *Centerfold*, in which a classroom of high school girls dance in their underwear?

One parent who didn't like what her children were seeing on MTV was Tipper Gore, whose husband, Al Gore, was an influential senator from Tennessee who would later become vice president. In 1985 Tipper Gore founded the Parents' Music Resource Center and commenced a campaign to add a parental code to compact discs (CDs), warning parents of explicit content in the lyrics. She proposed that the code be modeled after the ratings system adopted by the movie industry in the 1960s. By the late 1980s, Gore extended her campaign to music videos. "It's the youth market they're going after," she complained. "We're talking about the impact on young children and pre-teens."[20]

In 1988 Gore called on MTV to cluster its most explicit music videos in time periods late at night, when young children would least likely be watching them. MTV executives resisted, calling her efforts a form of censorship. MTV exec-

utives argued that the network maintained its own code of standards—the network had, after all, refused to air *Justify My Love*. "We think if they make it through [our] standards, they should be on MTV,"[21] insisted Marshall Cohen, MTV vice president. Furthermore, Cohen argued, rock music and its videos were, by their nature, controversial; historically, the people who make music have pushed the limits of what mainstream critics find acceptable.

For MTV and other music video programmers, public opinion was clearly running against them. In 1996 Congress passed the US Telecommunications Act, enabling televisions to be manufactured with the so-called V-chip, empowering parents to block programming. Moreover, in 1997 the TV industry finally gave in to pressure and adopted a voluntary code of guidelines, describing the content of the programming viewers were about to see—including the content of music videos.

Tipper Gore and Susan Baker (left to right) testify before a US Senate committee discussing government regulation of objectionable music lyrics in 1985.

What Became of the Buggles?

The Buggles's video for the song "Video Killed the Radio Star" launched MTV in 1981. Ironically, the video didn't do much to help the Buggles. The group was never able to capitalize on its landmark place in music video history.

The British duet was formed in 1979 by Trevor Horn and Geoff Downes. "Video Killed the Radio Star" was released that year as a single and hit the top of the charts in many European countries, but did not appear on an album (titled *The Age of Plastic*) until 1980. Later that year, after recording their second album, Downes and Horn decided to break up their band after receiving an offer to join Yes, a very popular rock group from the era. Both musicians toured with Yes, but Horn soon left the band and became a busy music producer for some major recording stars, including Paul McCartney, Rod Stewart, and Tina Turner. In addition, he often performed for those stars as a backup vocalist and keyboard player.

In 1998 Horn and Downes reunited for a single performance at a London nightclub. They performed one song: "Video Killed the Radio Star."

The Buggles—Trevor Horn and Geoff Downes—were never able to capitalize on having the first video ever played on MTV.

No Longer Music Television

By the 1990s, the quality of the content of music videos had grown to be less of a concern for MTV because what had been born as an all-music video network had started featuring nonmusic programming. Among these programs were animated shows such as *Beavis and Butthead* and reality shows including *The Real World* and *Jackass*. The new owners of MTV, the entertainment company Viacom, had launched additional cable networks to carry the music videos that the flagship station no longer had room to air. Among them were VH1, which is aimed at an audience older than the MTV demographic, as well as VH1 Classic, VH1 Soul, MTV2, MTV Hits, MTV Jams, and mtvU. Meanwhile, the Internet has also emerged as a platform for music videos—many artists premiere their videos on their own websites, while millions of fans each day watch their favorite videos on YouTube and similar Internet sites.

Three decades after its founding, MTV is no longer the music network. In fact, in 2010 the network quietly dropped the words "Music Television" from the MTV logo. Now, MTV's programming includes such shows as *Jersey Shore*, *Teen Mom*, and *Awkward*—mostly reality shows and teen-oriented dramas. Still, there is no debating that MTV facilitated the art and business of music videos, opening the way for a new medium of entertainment to find a wide audience.

CHAPTER 3

The Art of Music Videos

W hen music videos first made their debut, they provided a new outlet for pop music performers to reach their fans. But they also represented an opportunity for performers and producers to showcase their talents as visual artists. Many turned to surrealism, a form of art that first became popular nearly a century ago.

A recent example of surrealism can be found in the 2011 video released by teenage hip-hop star Mac Miller for his hit song "Frick Park Market." As the story unfolds, fans see the rapper taking on the role of a sandwich maker in a rundown Pittsburgh, Pennsylvania, deli. Miller works behind the counter, making a turkey sandwich. As he finishes, Miller reaches across the counter to hand the sandwich to a customer—a decidedly nerdy dude wearing a frizzy blond wig, dark-rimmed glasses, and a 1970s-style tuxedo. It doesn't take long for the viewer to realize that the customer is also played by Miller.

As Miller, the cook, launches into a rap about his life, he is joined in a duet by his tuxedo-wearing alter ego. As the video moves on, the camera finds Miller, the deli worker, taking out the trash; outside the deli, he notices a blue, glowing doorway standing on the sidewalk. He hesitates for a moment, then pushes his way through the door, where he finds a world lit by eerie black light. Dancers dabbed with

Day-Glo paint gyrate to Miller's raps. Miller's frizzy-haired clone can also be found in this new world, along with dancers dressed as giant rabbits, bears, long-beaked storks, and human skeletons—all moving to the beat as Miller raps, over and over again, the same lyrics inviting his friends into the market to join this strange world. As the video ends, everyone joins Miller in a rousing finale—back behind the counter of the deli.

Miller explains that the idea for the video was to introduce a weird, alternate universe to the fans. "The concept of that, it was like a garden of girls and black light," Miller says. "All these girls looked so sweet and trippy . . . My idea was to put all the girls in onesie bathing suits and make them look like synchronized swimmers and put caps on 'em, but we just made 'em look trippy."[22]

The Birth of Surrealism

Mac Miller may have described his vision as "trippy," but what he was really describing was surrealism—a form of art that has fascinated, confused, and confounded art fans for years due to its unbridled devotion to weirdness. Miller's video was produced to help promote the rapper's debut album, *Blue Slide Park*. The video for "Frick Park Market" was posted on YouTube in August 2011. Within three months, more than 7 million of Miller's fans watched it on YouTube, while others found it elsewhere on the Internet.

Miller's video takes his fans into a surreal world—where real-life people mingle with characters found only in the imagination. Surrealism is an artistic movement that first found popularity in the 1920s. The term was concocted in 1917 by French poet Guillaume Apollinaire after he attended a production of the ballet *Parade*. The ballet features all manner of make-believe characters, including winged horses, harlequins, and Indian mystics. Some of the costumes were made of cardboard, while the orchestra members were often called on to perform the score using some unusual musical instruments—among them a typewriter, siren, pistol, and foghorn.

Apollinaire was asked to provide the text for the ballet's

program; in describing the ballet's unusual features, he used the word *surrealisme*—in English, super realism. Eventually, the term was shortened to surrealism. Essentially, surrealism is the merger of images drawn entirely from the artist's imagination with images that can be found in real life. In 1924 French poet André Breton defined surrealism when he said, "Art, daily life and love become poetry when they tend toward a fusion of the imaginary and the real."[23]

Experiments in Abstract Art

Surrealism was born in the years immediately following World War I as many visual artists started experimenting with different forms of abstract art. The Spanish painter Pablo Picasso pioneered the "cubist" movement, dissecting images and breaking them down to their simplest parts, then rearranging them into abstract form. That is why the cubist portraits painted by Picasso and others often show hands, ears, legs, arms, heads, and other body parts depicted out of place—eyes may be stacked atop one another or perhaps an eye would be embedded in a nose.

Another important abstract movement of the era was Dada—in French, *dada* means hobbyhorse. Pioneered by French artists Jean Arp and Marcel Duchamp, the Dadaists took a playful attitude toward serious art. Duchamp, for example, reproduced the *Mona Lisa*, the famous sixteenth-century portrait by Italian painter Leonardo da Vinci, but finished off his version of da Vinci's masterpiece by painting a mustache on the model. Arp worked in the mediums of painting and sculpture. He was known to compose pictures by slathering a layer of glue onto a sheet of paper, then tearing paper into scraps and letting them fall onto the glue, forming images as they adhered to the sticky surface. His sculptures tended to be roundish—taking parts of his models' bodies and emphasizing them as spheres and orbs.

Cubism, Dada, and other abstract movements were all factors in the birth of surrealism. Among the leading surrealists of the era were Belgian René Magritte, German Max Ernst, American Emmanuel Radnitzky (known more familiarly as Man Ray), and Spaniard Joan Miró. Among their works were Magritte's 1937 *Portrait of Edward James*, in which a man looks into a mirror to see the back of his own head, and Miró's *Harlequin's Carnival*; painted in 1925, the latter work depicts a cacophony of characters, including insects, fish, mermaids, musicians, and clowns, rendered in an abstract scene. Man Ray worked as both a painter and photographer; one of his most familiar surreal images is the photograph "Present," depicting an ordinary household iron standing on end, but with nails protruding from the flat side that would ordinarily be expected to smooth the wrinkles out of clothing. Another typical example of surrealism is Ernst's *The Elephant of Celebes*, in which a robot-like elephant follows closely behind a headless nude. Ernst produced the painting in 1921.

The unquestioned leader of the surrealism movement, though, was Spaniard Salvador Dalí, who produced dozens of surreal paintings over a career that spanned some seven decades. His most famous image is *The Persistence of Memory*; painted in 1931, the work depicts floppy clock faces that melt over a dark, barren, and dismal landscape.

The leading figure in the surrealism movement, Salvador Dalí, poses with his oil painting Movies *in 1943.*

Surrealism on the Screen

Surrealism would soon move beyond the painted image. Filmmakers adopted surrealism as a medium to tell their stories. One of the first surreal films was the 1931 French movie *L'Age d'Or*—in English, *The Golden Age*—which was directed by Salvador Dalí and Spanish filmmaker Luis Buñuel. The movie has no real plot—it is a series of unrelated vignettes strung together that tell the vague story of two lovers kept apart by a variety of circumstances. The film shows scenes of stinging scorpions, chanting archbishops, a soldier—played by Max Ernst—forced into a life of begging, the arrests of the lovers by French policemen, a boy shot by his father, and a symphony conductor suddenly stopping a concert because he has a headache. "A kind of dream, which first of all should make you dream, the film defies all logic, even symbolic," says surrealist painter and author René Passeron. "It sets an example of an absolute and gratuitous freedom of the imagination."[24]

When the movie was first shown in Paris, France, it stirred controversy, as audiences simply didn't understand the concept behind surrealism—that it was an example of imagination permitted to run wild but still centered in the real world. Activists from the Croix de Feu, an extreme right-wing political movement of the era, vandalized the theater where *L'Age d'Or* was playing and slashed paintings by Miró, Ernst, and Dalí that were on display in the lobby. Finally, the film was banned by the French government and would not be shown in public again until 1981.

Across the Atlantic Ocean, American filmmakers were also influenced by the surrealism movement, but, knowing the tastes of their conservative audiences, knew that a film like *L'Age d'Or* would never find wide acceptance in America. Still, they managed to work elements of surrealism into their plots. The 1933 horror-adventure film *King Kong* is regarded as a landmark in American filmmaking. The now familiar story tells of an American movie crew discovering the existence of a giant ape (and dinosaurs!) on a remote island in the Pacific Ocean. After the ape, known as Kong, snatches the beautiful heroine, the filmmakers pursue the ape and manage to sneak her away. They are also able to capture Kong by drugging him into a stupor. The giant ape is shipped back to New York City and put on display, but breaks away and wreaks havoc on the city.

There is no question that the movie is a story of adventure and, given the limited technology available at the time, it blazed new trails in the use of special effects. But there are also scenes in *King Kong* that are clearly surreal. For example, in what is perhaps the film's most famous scene, the giant ape—a product of a scriptwriter's vivid imagination—stands atop the Empire State Building, an actual man-made

structure, swatting at fighter planes as they try to shoot him down. In that scene, the make-believe was merged into a scene from the real world, creating a surreal image. Says film historian Cynthia Marie Erb, "It is well known that the surrealists held *King Kong* in esteem because of its nightmarish qualities."[25]

King Kong's most famous scene, atop the Empire State Building, is an example of how US filmmakers were influenced by surrealism.

Music Videos Embrace Surrealism

Musicals would also embrace surreal scenes. Fred Astaire's tap dance in front of nine versions of himself in *Blue Skies* was certainly a surreal image. So were the hippo ballerinas twirled through the air by their crocodile suitors in *Fantasia*. Astaire took another plunge into surrealism when he danced on the walls and ceiling of a room in the 1951 film *Royal Wedding*. To pull off the stunt, the filmmakers constructed a set that rotated as the camera stood still. As the room spun

Sledgehammer and Surrealism

In 1992 Rolling Stone magazine named the surreal video for "Sledgehammer" as number one on its list of the top one hundred music videos of all time. The video features singer Peter Gabriel riding a rollercoaster, watching a train circle his head, having his face re-created with vegetables, and witnessing a cabaret act performed by a pair of headless chickens. The video employs live-action filming as well as animation and the use of puppets.

The 1986 video, which took a week to film, spans five minutes. "I was very uncomfortable at times," Gabriel says. "I remember well having an animated, sky-painted frame across my face and spending hours under a glass covered with fish stinking in the hot lights. . . . I think the success of the video grew out of great ideas [and] an excellent team."

Quoted in Jim Farber and Glenn Kenny. "The Top 100 Music Videos." *Rolling Stone*, October 14, 1992, p. 65.

below him, Astaire went through his steps. The scene that resulted showed Astaire seemingly in defiance of gravity. In later years, there was the 1979 movie *All That Jazz*, a biography of Broadway choreographer Bob Fosse, which includes plenty of singing and dancing but which also contains some surreal scenes as the protagonist carries on a running conversation with a white-veiled angel.

As the first music videos went into production, artists and their producers realized surrealism was an ideal vehicle to illustrate music in a video format. An early example of a surreal music video can be found in the video produced for the song "All the Machines," a cut on the 1984 comeback album *Software* by 1960s-era rocker Grace Slick. The video starts out with rapid-fire drumming, singing, and dancing by characters costumed as prehistoric cave dwellers. Soon these characters are transformed into a modern setting, surrounded by TV sets, vacuum cleaners, and digital clocks, as

well as several other weird technological devices that seem to serve no purpose.

During the video, Slick sings about how machines appear to have taken over people's lives. As the video moves on to its finale, the cave people find themselves worshipping the machines that are now so vital to what was once their simple and peaceful existence. Clearly, the concept for the video is based in surrealism: In the real Stone Age, cave dwellers would never come across TV sets or vacuum cleaners; meanwhile, in the modern age, people don't live in caves or use vacuum cleaners to clean their cave floors. "Inasmuch as any element can come to the fore, the world that a video depicts can become very strange," says Arizona State University film professor Carol Vernallis. "Some of music video's excitement stems from the sense that anything can happen."[26]

Another rock group of the era that embraced surrealism is the Grateful Dead, which continues to enjoy a cult following of dedicated fans known as Deadheads. In 1987 the group released a video for its single "Hell in a Bucket," which features many surreal scenes—including vocalist Bob Weir encountering two horned devils who take him on a cruise in a pink Cadillac while various circus performers provide entertainment along the way.

Rejecting Surrealism

Of course, over the years there have been some artists who have refused to employ surreal images in their videos. Veteran rocker Bruce Springsteen prefers that his videos simply feature his onstage performances—although occasionally with a twist. For the video for Springsteen's 1984 single "Dancing in the Dark," the scenario is nothing more than a concert performance as Springsteen and his group, the E Street Band, play the song in front of a packed arena.

When Springsteen has agreed to film a non-concert scenario for a video, the plot usually depicts a simple story that accompanies the music. For his 1993 song "Streets of Philadelphia," the camera slowly follows Springsteen as he strolls along lonely city streets, singing of alienation. The song would go on to win an Academy Award for Best Original Song for the film *Philadelphia*, which relates the story of a young lawyer dying of AIDS.

Earlier, Springsteen made a video for his 1985 hit song "I'm on Fire," in which he plays an auto mechanic returning a car to a wealthy woman he loves. Springsteen's character knows she would never accept him as an equal because of the differences in their social positions, which is the theme

of the song he sings as he drives the repaired car to her mansion. Even with this lack of pyrotechnics often found in other music videos, the video for "I'm on Fire" received critical acclaim. In 1985 it won the MTV Video Music Award for Best Male Video. And it was completely lacking in surreal images.

Bruce Springsteen rejected surrealism in videos such as Dancing in the Dark, *which was taped in 1984.*

Spears Goes "Toxic"

Still, even as artists like Bruce Springsteen continue to command huge audiences for their performances as well as their videos, there is no question that many of today's performers rely heavily on surrealism to provide a visual impact for their music. Unlike Springsteen, most top performers are more likely to adopt a scenario for their videos akin to that of "Toxic," a 2004 release by Britney Spears. In the video, Spears starts her surreal adventure as a sexy flight attendant who seduces one of the passengers, then transforms into a dancer wearing the sheerest of diamond-studded bodysuits,

CGI and Music Videos

The art of computer-generated imaging, or CGI, is a staple of many Hollywood animated films, like *Shrek* and *Toy Story*. One of the first showcases of CGI animation was a music video for the 1987 song "Money for Nothing" by the rock band Dire Straits.

The video features concert footage of the band, but also several scenes of two computer-generated TV repairmen enjoying the music. They also act out the lyrics described by the band and even join in the performance. The animation was provided by Ian Anderson, one of the pioneers of CGI production. It took Anderson nearly a month to create the CGI animation for the four-minute video. "Ian just lived in the [production] room," says Steve Barron, who directed the video. "I gave him all the storyboards and he was there literally 24 hours a day, working three days straight then sleeping for eight hours. . . . We couldn't do it any other way because no one else could do it."

Quoted in David Knight, Neon Kelly, Owen Lawrence, and Sharon Steinbach. "25 Videos That Changed the World." *Music Week*, September 2006, p. 23.

changing next into a motorcycle rider zooming through city streets.

Arriving at a chemical factory, she breaks in to steal a vial of poison, then escapes through a wall of flames and dances through shooting laser beams (performing a backflip to make good her escape). The camera then cuts to the vertical wall of a skyscraper, finding Spears scaling the edifice, in defiance of gravity, in a search for her unfaithful lover—whom she ultimately poisons. Finally, the camera cuts back to the interior of the airliner, where Spears, as the flight attendant, ends the video with a wink toward the camera as a flock of doves trails behind.

All of this action occurs within the video's three minutes and thirty-two seconds. National Public Radio music critic Amy Schriefer says surreal videos like *Toxic* should be judged solely on how much fun they are to watch. She says,

Spears in "Toxic" is out to have a good time on her own terms. The campy video for "Toxic" captures the moment perfectly: Spears gleefully adopts different alter-egos and traipses through . . . tropes of femininity to steal a poison, ride a motorcycle, steward an airplane and literally cover herself in diamonds. She's sexy and comfortable, even when wearing nothing but diamond-encrusted skin. . . . This is genuine fun.[27]

Katy Perry in Candy Land

Other pop stars have followed Britney Spears into surrealism. In 2010 Katy Perry released the single "California Gurls." The song's lyrics provide an homage to the free spirit of the young girls who live in California, but nothing depicted in the "California Gurls" video resembles anything that can be found in the actual state of California. Instead, the video features miniaturized versions of the singer and her dancers as they negotiate their way through a land resembling a Candy Land game, where the candy, whipped cream, ice cream, cake frosting, and other sweets are all real. Along the way, Perry encounters an army of unfriendly Gummi Bears, frees one friend from a gooey bubble of gum, and breaks into a block of green Jell-O to emancipate another. She also encounters friendly snakes made out of peppermint sticks, reclines on a pink cloud of cotton candy, and makes friends with a grumpy gingerbread man. The hip-hop star Snoop Dogg, playing the villain, joins in with some raps about how he plans to take over this sugary wonderland. But Perry prevails, drowning Snoop in a deluge of whipped cream, and the girls of this candy-coated version of California win the day.

MTV critic James Montgomery found the video lots of fun. "The 'Gurls' video . . . is three minutes and 54 seconds of deliciously gaudy, delightfully ridiculous eye candy, a sugar-coated overload of confectionery gone haywire, cotton-candy clouds, gingerbread paths and Gummi Bears with bad attitudes," he wrote. "It is bright and brash and

The Real "California Girls"

While Katy Perry may have scored a hit with "California Gurls," the name of Perry's song should not be confused with a true rock-and-roll classic: "California Girls," recorded in 1965 by the Beach Boys. "California Girls" was a major hit and is regarded as the signature song for the group. Its lyrics tell the story of a world traveler who has concluded that the most beautiful women on the planet can be found in California.

The Beach Boys performed the song on TV numerous times, but never made a video of "California Girls" in what was, of course, the pre-video age. However, in 1985 rocker David Lee Roth included a cover of "California Girls" on his album *Crazy from the Heat*. And Roth did produce a video for the song. Eschewing surrealism, the three-minute video mostly shows Roth frolicking on the beach with bikini-clad models.

very likely to give you a toothache. Like the song, there is nothing understated about it."[28]

The dedication that stars like Perry and Spears have shown toward depicting surreal worlds for their videos illustrates that even nearly a century after surrealism surfaced as a form of art, it has found what may be an everlasting home in music videos. As Perry makes her way through a land of candy canes, or as Spears defies gravity in search of an unfaithful boyfriend, or even as Mac Miller hands his alter ego a turkey sandwich, the art of surrealism has proven that it can still provide inspiration to the video stars of the twenty-first century.

Katy Perry performs at the MuchMusic Video Awards in Toronto, Canada, in 2010, using a set similar to her California Gurls *video.*

CHAPTER 4

When Music Videos Make Political and Social Statements

C yndi Lauper was just beginning her rise to pop stardom in 1983 when she recorded the hit "Girls Just Wanna Have Fun." The song and its video made a statement about young women of the era—that it was a time of female empowerment and they should be willing to defy their parents and be less concerned about schoolwork, finding jobs, and starting families of their own.

"When she comes home for dinner, Cyndi gives her exasperated parents an impromptu lecture about the modern women's wants and needs,"[29] says music critic Saul Austerlitz. In fact, Lauper declares in the song that youth is a golden time—a time in which young women should be enjoying themselves. In the video, one of the most popular aired on MTV during the 1980s, Lauper gathers her girlfriends together and leads them on an electrifying conga line over city streets.

As the video continues, the parade of young women gets longer—and even picks up some boys—until the party finally ends back in Lauper's home. The message of the song and its video have never lost traction among fans; the song remains as popular today as it was when it was originally recorded. In 2008 Miley Cyrus included a cover of "Girls Just Wanna Have Fun" on her CD *Breakout*. Cyrus also filmed a video for the song, but she declined to add a visual dimension to the song's statement. The video was shot in a studio and simply displayed Cyrus and her band performing the song—letting the lyrics speak for themselves.

Lauper's video, produced so early in music video history, established an important precedent: In the coming years, music videos would serve as much more than just vehicles to display the talents of the performers or the artistic abilities of the videos' producers and directors. Many performers have recognized the power of the video to make political and social statements.

Too Much Fun

Sometimes music videos portray more serious subjects. Such was the case in the video for Madonna's 1986 hit "Papa Don't Preach," which spent several weeks ranked as the number-one single on the pop charts. The video depicts Madonna as she walks the lonely streets of the city, rehearsing what she plans to tell her father: that she is pregnant and intends to keep the baby. After visiting her boyfriend and breaking the news to him, Madonna's character finally confronts her father, telling him of the pregnancy. At the end of the video, she learns just how much her father loves her when he takes her in his arms in a warm embrace.

In many ways, the video marked a sharp departure from what fans were used to seeing in Madonna's on-screen performances. In most of her videos Madonna promoted her sex appeal, usually strutting through her tightly choreographed dances in stiletto heels and barely there costumes. Throughout most of the video for "Papa Don't Preach," the singer wanders through the streets of the city dressed in blue jeans and a demure striped blouse.

The song as well as the video sparked a firestorm of

Cyndi Lauper made one of the most popular videos of the 1980s for the song "Girls Just Wanna Have Fun."

Madonna films her controversial Papa Don't Preach *video in 1986.*

controversy as pro-choice and anti-abortion rights groups spent weeks debating Madonna's message. Groups opposed to abortion rights insisted that the pop star's message contained in the song and video was one of a rejection of abortion. Said Susan Carpenter-McMillan, president of the California chapter of Feminists for Life in America, "Abortion is readily available on every street corner for

When Madonna Killed Her Own Video

Madonna has earned the reputation as an edgy performer willing to stand up to censorship, but in 2003 she agreed to pull the video for her single "American Life" for fear that she would be considered unpatriotic. At the time, America was embroiled in wars in Afghanistan and Iraq.

America's participation in the wars had divided the country, with many Americans particularly opposed to President George W. Bush's decision to invade Iraq. *American Life* includes many military-related images and ends as Madonna tosses a hand grenade at an actor portraying the president, who uses it to light a cigar. Before the video was released, though, Madonna decided to withhold it from broadcast on MTV and other music networks. The singer said she did not want to offend US troops, whom she supported. Said the singer, "Due to the volatile state of the world and out of sensitivity and respect to the armed forces, who I support and pray for, I do not want to risk offending anyone who might misinterpret the meaning of this video."

Later, a new version of the video was released. In the re-filmed—and much more tame version—Madonna sings the song in front of a changing backdrop of flags from different nations.

Quoted in Heather Havrilesky. "The Madonna Video You Can't See on MTV." Salon.com, April 3, 2003. www .salon.com/2003/04/03/madonna_6.

young women. Now, what Madonna is telling them is, 'Hey, there's an alternative.'"[30]

Misinterpreting Madonna's Message

But pro-choice groups weighed in as well, insisting that the song and its video contain a message of warning to girls. Early in the video, Madonna approaches her boyfriend, an auto mechanic. The video does not portray the moment when Madonna tells the boy of the pregnancy, but later the video shows the two lovers in a warm moment, suggesting that the boy approves and has agreed to support the baby. According to Alfred Moran, executive director of the New York branch of Planned Parenthood, the message of the video should be clear—that young people do not have the financial resources to raise a child, and by deciding to give birth to the baby the two young parents would be committing themselves to a lifetime of financial stress. Said Moran, "The message is that getting pregnant is cool and having the baby is the right thing and a good thing and don't listen to your parents, the school, anybody who tells you otherwise—don't preach to me Papa. The reality is that what Madonna is suggesting to teenagers is a path to permanent poverty."[31]

Meanwhile, liberal columnist Ellen Goodman, an abortion rights advocate, complained that the video actually glamorizes teen pregnancy. She pointed out that in the video, Madonna's boyfriend is a hunky dreamboat with a conscience and moral compass, while her father is loving, supportive, and even-tempered. She argued that few pregnant teenage girls would find similar support from their boyfriends or family members. "This happily-ever-after image has about as much to do with the reality of adolescent motherhood as Madonna's [shapely] figure has to do with pregnancy," Goodman said.[32]

As for Madonna, she insisted both groups misinterpreted her message. As in the song and video for "Girls Just Wanna Have Fun," Madonna contended that the message of "Papa Don't Preach" was about the empowerment of women. In the song and video, Madonna made it clear that it was her decision, and her decision alone, to give birth to the child. "Immediately [anti-abortion rights groups] are going to say I am advising every young girl to go out and get pregnant," says Madonna. "This song is really about a girl who is making a decision in her life."[33]

Fighting the Power

While pro-choice and anti-abortion rights advocates may have found themselves in a long debate over Madonna's message, there was no misinterpreting the message transmitted by the hip-hop group Public Enemy in its 1989 single "Fight the Power," which was included on the album *Fear of a Black Planet*. The song and its video express frustration with the pace of the civil rights movement, insisting that in the years since the 1964 US Civil Rights Act was adopted by Congress, African Americans had still not achieved full equality with whites.

The video was directed by African American film director Spike Lee, who had helmed several racially charged movies. In fact, Lee had used "Fight the Power" as the introductory music to his 1989 film *Do the Right Thing*, which tells the story of how a riot erupts in a racially mixed Brooklyn, New York, neighborhood.

Lee's video for "Fight the Power" opens with newsreel footage of the 1963 civil rights march on Washington, D.C., led by the Reverend Martin Luther King Jr. Some two hundred thousand people took part in the march, calling on Congress to end the so-called Jim Crow laws that denied equality to black Americans. The footage shows blacks marching together with whites in a spirit of unity. The narrator of the newsreel provides an upbeat message, predicting that change is in the air and that lawmakers in Washington intend to heed the desires of the crowd and adopt legislation guaranteeing equality to minorities.

The video then cuts quickly to the contemporary streets of Brooklyn, where Public Enemy is leading its own rally for racial equality. Led by rapper Chuck D, the message told by Public Enemy is much different than what the narrator conveyed back in 1963. Public Enemy tells the crowd that things have not changed, that black people still do not enjoy equality in America, and that it is time to stop talking and start fighting.

Lee's scenes of the crowd show unity among the demonstrators, to be sure, but they also show anger. Indeed, for one brief moment, the camera focuses on Tawana Brawley, who was at the center of a racially charged incident in 1987 when, at the age of fifteen, she claimed to have been raped by six white men, including members of the police force, in nearby Wappinger Falls, New York. An investigation later concluded that Brawley had not been assaulted—an outcome disputed by some black activists who charged that white officials had engineered a cover-up of the crime.

And so, nearly two decades before Americans elected Barack Obama the first African American president, race relations in American cities were often tense. Music historian Denise Sullivan says Public Enemy captured that mood in the video for "Fight the Power." She says,

Public Enemy was making its statement in the era when Michael Jackson went to visit Ronald and Nancy Reagan [the President and First Lady] in the White House and the economy was enjoying a boom time. But as Chuck D never fails to point out, the [era] meant hard times for another set of folks. Raising his voice in resistance, he was out there blowing the whistle on America the beautiful, a place where the idea of a holi-

Public Enemy shoots the politically charged video Fight the Power *with director Spike Lee (far right).*

day in honor of Dr. King could still be met with rejection. . . . Public Enemy set the bar high for the new age of protest music.[34]

The Gangsta Life

By the mid-1990s, the message from the hip-hop community had changed dramatically. Less concerned with equality, hip-hop artists were now rapping about violence and the "gangsta" lifestyle. This was the era in which some of

Coolio performs in Amsterdam, the Netherlands, in 1996. His breakthrough album told the story of a "gangsta" life.

rap music's biggest names, including Tupac Shakur and Christopher Wallace (known to his fans as Biggie Smalls and the Notorious B.I.G.), had been murdered in violent shooting incidents.

In 1995 hip-hop star Coolio told the story of the violent world of the gangsta life when he released the single "Gangsta's Paradise." It was a life that Coolio knew well, having grown up on the gang-infested streets of Compton, California. His father abandoned the family and his mother was addicted to drugs. To survive, he committed robberies and burglaries and was soon addicted to crack cocaine. After spending ten months in jail, he decided to give up drugs and clean up his life.

Coolio also started rapping, but with little success—in 1993, he was living on welfare. But one of his tapes made it to a New York producer, who recognized Coolio's talent. Coolio cut his first album of rap music, *It Takes a Thief*, in 1994; a year later he recorded his breakthrough album, *Gangsta's Paradise*, which featured the title song. (Coolio is accompanied on the single by the rhythm-and-blues singer known as L.V., whose real name is Larry Sanders.)

Finding Love with the Black Eyed Peas

In the months following the terrorist attacks of September 2001, Americans found themselves horrified by the loss of life and committed to a war on terrorism but also divided politically as many national leaders vowed to disregard human rights as they sought to protect the country against future terrorism. Amid this atmosphere, the Black Eyed Peas produced the 2003 single "Where is the Love?"

The video depicts the members of the group traveling throughout East Los Angeles, posting signs containing question marks on buildings, buses, and other public places, calling on people to put their anger aside and start showing one another love. Explained group member will.i.am, "We're going to inform the people what it is that we want them to know, how we think about life and how we live our life and what consumes our mind socially."

Quoted in George Lipsitz. *Footsteps in the Dark: The Hidden Histories of Popular Music.* Minneapolis: University of Minnesota Press, 2007, p. 270.

"Gangsta's Paradise" was included in the soundtrack for the film *Dangerous Minds*, a story in which a white teacher, portrayed by Michelle Pfeiffer, tries to connect with the African American students in an inner-city school. The song, with its haunting, pulsating beat, and its video, filmed mostly in shadows, turned out to be so popular that it is believed they are largely responsible for the success of the film.

There is no question, though, that Coolio was making a statement about the gangsta life in the video. In the scenario for the video, Pfeiffer again plays the role of the teacher, but remains mostly silent throughout the four-minute video as Coolio explains the gangsta life of drugs, guns, and violence. "If you live in the ghetto I come from, an element of life you dealt with every day was that you lived in the gangsta's paradise," Coolio says. "You didn't have to be one, but you had to walk down the same streets."[35]

Challenging Their Fans

The messages offered by Cyndi Lauper, Coolio, and Public Enemy could easily be interpreted by viewers. People who saw Madonna's video for "Papa Don't Preach" may have had their own ideas about what the pop star intended to say, but at least they found meaning in her words. Other artists have chosen to challenge their fans as well as critics, offering videos in which the themes are not always easy to understand.

In 2010 Lady Gaga and Beyoncé starred in a video version of Lady Gaga's song "Telephone." The song itself is lively dance music; the lyrics tell the simple story of a woman who doesn't want to interrupt a dance to take a telephone call. The video tells a much different story: At nine minutes in length—more of a brief film than a music video—the scenario depicts Lady Gaga being marched down a prison corridor, where she is tossed into a cell. Later she is led into an exercise yard draped in chains; her vision blocked by sunglasses made out of cigarettes. The video contains implied lesbian relations, use of the harshest of profanities, and the commission of mass murder. Finally, after escaping from prison, Lady Gaga and Beyoncé make their getaway in a pickup truck as the words "To Be Continued . . ." flash across the screen.

The video was embraced by fans of Lady Gaga as well as Beyoncé; posted on YouTube and other Internet sites, the video chalked up more than 15 million views in less than a week. "What I really wanted to do with this video is take a decidedly pop song, which on the surface has a quite shallow meaning, and turn it into something deeper,"[36] Lady Gaga said.

The Scary Female Monster

But what exactly are the messages that Lady Gaga means to convey in the video? According to Meghan Vicks, a doctoral student in comparative literature at the University of

Colorado, there are many political and social themes examined in the video for "Telephone." The prison scenes, she says, serve as a metaphor for the imprisoned identity of the protagonist. While chained and blinded by the cigarettes, Vicks says, Lady Gaga must struggle to break out—to find her own identity.

Jonas Akerlund, director of the video, says the video for "Telephone" also makes a statement about conditions in American prisons—inmates shackled in chains and cruel guards are all facts of life in prison. "We believe it is something that is happening in both men's and women's jails and it is part of the picture in our made-up prison world,"[37] he says.

In one scene Lady Gaga is wrapped in yellow crime scene tape—typically, such tape is imprinted with the words "Crime Scene—Do Not Cross." In wrapping the character in crime scene tape, Vicks believes Lady Gaga is making a

Lady Gaga and Beyoncé attend the MTV Video Music Awards in 2009. Their 2010 video Telephone *had more than 15 million views after just one week.*

Rihanna's Violent Video

Music videos have long been criticized by parents' groups and others for their sexual content, but complaints have also been raised about the violent content of videos. In 2011, when a video for Rihanna's song "Man Down" premiered on the TV network BET, the Parents Television Council called on the network to stop airing it. The reason: The video begins as Rihanna shoots a man in the head.

Rihanna defended the video, insisting that it made a statement about a woman's response to a man who had been abusing her. "We just wanted to hone in on a very serious matter that people are afraid to address, especially if you've been victimized in this scenario," said the singer. BET elected to continue airing the video, finding it in compliance with its code of standards for acceptable content.

Quoted in Fox News. "Rihanna Defends 'Man Down' Music Video: It's 'Art With a Message.'" June 3, 2011. www.foxnews.com/entertainment/2011/06/03/rihanna -defends-man-down-music-video-its-art-with-message.

definite political statement about society's refusal to accept women with criminal records. "A criminal female is any female that doesn't follow the rules, that doesn't fit the model as a good girl," Vicks says. "By wearing the crime scene tape she is making a statement about how our culture views the criminal female as frightening and more abnormal than a criminal male. Our culture thinks that there is something scarier about that sort of monster than a male monster."[38]

A Final Act of Rebellion

The video features several shots of both Lady Gaga and Beyoncé talking on the telephone—which is, after all, the overall theme of the original song. In the video, though, Vicks believes the telephone serves as another form of prison. "The telephone is a complicated tool," says Vicks. "Just like the prison, it can entrap us by dictating who we speak with."[39]

Near the end of the video, Lady Gaga poisons the food of all the customers in a diner. Meghan Vicks says that was the final act of rebellion against the society that put her in jail, and it is also the means under which Lady Gaga and Beyoncé are able to escape. Says Jonas Akerlund, "I am a little weird and a little untraditional in how and why I tell stories in music videos. But I enjoy the fact that people go deep and see things in my work because it means the music got out there and got some attention."[40]

If those are the political and social messages found in the video for "Telephone," there are many critics who question whether those are the correct messages to be sending to Lady Gaga's young fans. Sandy Rios, president of the conservative group Culture Campaign, does not believe the video for "Telephone" sends positive messages; she is particularly troubled by the near-nudity in some of the scenes as well as the implied sexuality. She suggests the video for "Telephone" is the type of film that could inspire sexual predators. "You may not watch it, your kids might not watch it, but I'm telling you, the man next door who's a sexual predator probably does watch it, and it has an effect on all of us," says Rios. "This should be outlawed and it should be banned, personally—there is a limit to what we should tolerate."[41] And critic Armond White of the *New York Press* describes the video for "Telephone" as "cruel and ugly," adding, "'Telephone' epitomizes the insanity of the contemporary pop mainstream."[42]

Lady Gaga's mixed messages in the video for "Telephone" illustrate how far music videos have come as vehicles for political and social expression since the days when Cyndi Lauper simply wanted to tell her parents to let her live her own life. In the meantime, they have sparked debate over such important public issues as civil rights, gang violence, and abortion. In the future, it is likely that music videos will continue to serve as vehicles for not only artistic expression but political and social messages as well.

CHAPTER 5

Making Music Videos at Home

Pop music took a definite turn toward the weird in the late 1970s when Devo first took the stage, mostly in new-wave clubs in the Los Angeles, California, area. The five Devo musicians wore costumes resembling yellow nylon space suits. Their headgear resembled flowerpots turned upside down. Their activities onstage were highly choreographed as they leapt about in sync. As for the music, it was frenetic and electronic, while the vocals were barked in short, angry bursts. "The group's crazed energy, athletic approach, obsessive manner and highly developed concept made for a show as intriguing as it was disturbing," wrote *Los Angeles Times* music critic Richard Cromelin after seeing Devo perform. "Also hilarious."[43]

Devo brought something more to the stage than just its unique brand of pop music: As Devo made the rounds of California's new-wave clubs, the group often projected homemade films onto a screen set up onstage. Surreal in style, one of the first films portrayed the Devo musicians in an escape from an Orwellian society loosely based on the plot of *The Prisoner*, a suspenseful TV series from the late 1960s. As the Devo band members performed their roles in the short films, their music played in the background.

Audiences responded and the films became a big part of Devo's act. At many of its performances, Devo would play

the films first before band members took the stage. The Devo musicians found that the films would excite the crowds and help build up toward the moment of drama when the band took the stage. Said band member Mark Mothersbaugh, "We [can] get a sneak preview because we can hear the audience's response to our movies before we come out."[44]

Devo would go on to become a popular group during the 1980s, recording many hit CDs. Devo's videos—now produced by professional filmmakers—were aired on MTV and other cable channels. Indeed, soon after recording its first two albums, *Q: Are We Not Men? A: We Are Devo!* and *Duty Now for the Future*, Devo signed a contract with a major entertainment company, Time-Life Books, to market its music videos to a national audience.

Devo, in their trademark red hats, perform in 1981.

Success on Treadmills

When Devo was first starting out, though, MTV had not yet gone on the air. And although other TV channels were featuring music videos, new and unknown groups like Devo were rarely given airtime. Moreover, an off-the-wall group like Devo would be hard-pressed to find backers willing to foot the cost of expensive music videos.

So the Devo band members made their first videos on their own, recording them on film instead of videotape, and using the films to add a unique element to their live stage shows. As such, Devo blazed a trail that has been followed in the ensuing decades by many new and unknown groups: Using their own sound and video recording equipment, many groups are able to create their own videos. And thanks to the Internet, musicians can make them available to fans and create interest in their music. Some of these homemade videos have gone viral on the Internet, leading to lucrative recording contracts for these talented musicians.

One such case was *Here It Goes Again*, a homemade video produced by the rock band OK Go. The video was easy to produce: It consisted of a single camera focused on a group of treadmills. Band members danced across the treadmills while the audio played a recording of the song. After uploading the video onto YouTube, the video for "Here It Goes

OK Go re-create their innovative video performance using treadmills for "Here It Goes Again" during the 2006 MTV Video Music Awards.

Again" went viral, capturing more than 15 million views within a few months. Moreover, the video won a Grammy Award in 2007 and helped OK Go, which had been a modestly successful band, score a major hit. Reported the Viral Video Chart, a British-based website that reviews web-based content, "There's nothing like watching four full-grown men execute a perfectly choreographed dance routine. Especially if the said dance routine incorporates treadmills, and the said men are geek-rock quadruplets OK Go."[45]

Using 16mm Film

A major reason that bands like OK Go can make their own music videos today is the relatively low cost of high-quality video recording equipment. For a few hundred dollars, an amateur videographer can purchase a high-definition digital video camera and, with another $100 or so, obtain video processing software that can enable the videographer to edit the footage and even add special effects on a home computer. The finished video can now be burned onto DVDs or uploaded onto the Internet.

Years ago, producing homemade music videos was a much more expensive proposition. Back in the 1970s Devo used 16mm movie gear—including cameras, lights, and sound recording equipment. The 16mm format—in which the film has a side-to-side measurement of sixteen millimeters—is twice the size of 8mm movie film, the type of film popular in the 1960s, used by people who owned home movie cameras to record vacations, children's birthday parties, weddings, and similar family events. The 16mm stock is, however, much smaller than the 35mm format used by professional filmmakers to produce Hollywood-style films, but 16mm film is still wide enough to record the type of detail that helps make the action on film come alive.

Nevertheless, even 16mm gear could cost several thousand dollars. It was cheaper to rent the equipment, but operating 16mm equipment took a certain amount of expertise. It also took expertise—and the proper equipment—to properly edit the film after the scenes were shot.

And the chemical process of developing the film could also be expensive, particularly if the footage was shot in color. Developing movie film is not a process easily accomplished in a basement darkroom; typically, it has to be processed by a professional lab. During the 1970s not many garage bands had the resources to produce their own music videos on 16mm film.

The Arrival of Videotape

The cost of production would start dropping in price in the mid-1970s, thanks to some technology developed in Japan. In 1976 the Japanese electronics company JVS introduced the VHS format in videotape—VHS stands for video home system. Now consumers could buy tape on cassettes and insert them into videocassette players, which were connected to their TV sets by cables. Hollywood studios made their films available on tape so consumers could enjoy them at home. Blank cassettes could be obtained by consumers who could record their favorite programs right off the TV or even make their own movies shot on home video cameras, replacing the old 8mm cameras.

Actually, videotape had been in use for many years prior to the development of the VHS format—a much wider format of the tape was typically used by TV news crews. Broadcast news organizations found the instant recording and playback capabilities of videotape enabled them to broadcast news events much more quickly than if they had to record the action on 16mm film, which, of course, had to be developed and edited back in the studio.

For amateur rock-and-roll bands, the introduction of the VHS videotape format made it easier and cheaper to produce their own music videos—but, at first, not too much cheaper. A good VHS camera could still cost $1,000 or more. The videocassettes were relatively inexpensive, costing just a few dollars each, but it took an expert and high-quality equipment to edit videotape, particularly if the bands wanted to add special effects. Of course, none of this could be done on home computers, which were just beginning to show up on the consumer market in the 1980s. Indeed, the home computers of the era, such as the Commodore 64 or Apple II, could do little more than produce text documents and play rudimentary games.

Learning How to Direct

Still, some independent bands managed to scrape together the resources to produce their own videotape-based music videos. In 1981 the Chicago, Illinois, band Phil 'n' the Blanks produced a video of its single "PRL-8-53," a song from the band's self-produced vinyl 45. The band received a lot of help from a professional videographer, Joe Federici, who produced the video in his free time. Federici had been working for corporate clients at the time, making sales videos and similar business-related productions. Federici said he volunteered to help Phil 'n' the Blanks and other local bands to gain experience in music video production, hop-

The Music Video App

Smartphones and tablet computers are now so sophisticated that software companies believe such devices are all a would-be rock star needs to make his or her own music video. The devices typically include video cameras and microphones. Now, a software company has produced a downloadable app that helps people produce their own music videos.

The app provides a template that serves as the foundation on which the images and music can be added. Once the template is opened, the app provides instructions on how to add the images and music. In 2011 the game producer Harmonix announced it had produced VidRhythm, a music video app for Apple smartphones and tablet computers. The company said it had also obtained permission from some major recording artists to use their music in the app, meaning fans have access to some three thousand songs if they are unable to make their own music.

ing to one day become a full-time music video director. "I always preferred entertainment to industrials,"[46] he said.

Phil 'n' the Blanks couldn't convince the national TV music programs to play the tape, but the band sent its self-produced video to a number of local clubs, which booked the band for gigs after viewing its performance. "It's a tool that we can have any time we play,"[47] said Phil Bimstein, a member of Phil 'n' the Blanks.

Federici was not alone in his desire to learn the techniques and styles of music video production. During this pre-digital era, many future music video directors made their first productions on videotape because that was the equipment available to them at the time. Adam Powell, who directs the videos for British rap star Tinchy Snyder and other British stars, says he learned to direct by using a video camera to record his friend's skateboarding stunts on VHS tape. "When I was around 16 or 17, me and my friend Kenny were skateboarding a lot," says Powell. "I was at college . . . but instead of working on course work we were just skating. Kenny had an idea that we should take his step-dad's old VHS camera and make some videos of him at the skate park. That's kind of how it got started, with him skating on a mini-ramp and me following around with a VHS camera."[48]

Soulja Boy Scores Big

Videocassette cameras have since been replaced by digital video cameras. And bands no longer have to mail their videos to club owners—they need only upload them onto the Internet. Indeed, now that digital equipment is available at relatively low prices, nearly any band can record its performances and hope to find a wide audience on the Internet. Some Internet-savvy performers have found ways to make Internet exposure work for them, snagging lucrative recording contracts or concert dates after record company executives or promoters see the number of views their videos receive on YouTube and similar sites.

In 2007 the rap star DeAndre Way, known to his fans as Soulja Boy, uploaded his homemade videos onto YouTube, MySpace, and a number of other sites, cleverly cross-promoting his videos from site to site and establishing his own webpage. "I started uploading videos of me promoting my music," he says. "Most of them were just me acting a fool, but in others I was acting like I was a real rapper—telling people my album was about to drop soon."[49]

This intense self-promotion helped him develop a base of fans. "I was so famous on YouTube and MySpace that people started booking me for shows," he says. "Every time I did a show in a new city, people knew my songs. It showed me the true power of the Internet."[50] Soon, Soulja Boy signed with a major label and, within three years of producing his first homemade video, the rap star had recorded three hit albums and was chalking up earnings of $7 million a year in record sales royalties and concert fees.

Soulja Boy, left, who started out uploading his own videos to the web in 2007, and 50 Cent on the set of their music video Mean Mug *in 2010.*

Waiting for Lightning to Strike

Other bands see the success scored by Soulja Boy and OK Go and believe they can achieve similar results, so they make their own videos and quickly upload them onto the Internet. In 2011 the band Infinity Hour—composed mostly of high school students from the Detroit, Michigan, suburb of Farmington Hills—produced a video for its song "She Finally Knows Why." The scenario for the video involves the band's interpretation of the *Little Red Riding Hood* fairy tale.

Guitarist Jared Bentley said production of the four-minute video was much more difficult than the band members expected. In fact, it took three days and multiple takes shot amid a wooded landscape before band members were satisfied with the footage. "There were so many options available, it was awesome," said Bentley. "We also all

"Pump It" and the Navy

In 2006 the Black Eyed Peas released the single "Pump It," a song that incorporates the fast-paced instrumental piece "Misirlou," best known as the theme music for the 1994 movie thriller *Pulp Fiction*. A year after the Black Eyed Peas released the song and its video, crew members of the US Navy aircraft carrier *Abraham Lincoln* produced their own music video of the song, using personnel aboard the carrier. The scenario for the video essentially shows the servicemen and servicewomen performing their duties while lip-syncing the lyrics to "Pump It" and occasionally breaking into dance or playing musical instruments. Above the action on the flight deck, Navy jets zoom overhead.

The Navy certainly took notice, particularly after the video was uploaded onto YouTube and scored nearly a million views—much more than the typical Navy recruiting video. Navy officials wondered whether the *Abraham Lincoln*'s version of "Pump It" helped spark an interest in young people toward enlisting in the service. "This is how people are getting their information," said Vice Admiral Mark Edwards. "You can tell your story on Google. You can tell your story on YouTube. It is such a powerful concept."

Quoted in Gidget Fuentes. "Homemade Videos Draw Target Audience: Sailors' Amateur Spoofs, Not Ad-Agency Pitches, Reaching Key Pool of Recruits." *Navy Times*, March 5, 2007, p. 18+.

US Navy personnel created a popular video to a song by the Black Eyed Peas—seen here during the band's 2011 Super Bowl halftime show—aboard an aircraft carrier.

got to know each other a lot better because it was the longest we've been together for one period of time, so it was a ton of fun."[51] Within a month of uploading the video to YouTube, *She Finally Knows Why* had been seen by about ten thousand fans. Following the production of the video, band members said they were making plans to record a full CD and produce additional videos.

Clearly, Infinity Hour is still looking for the type of success found by Soulja Boy and OK Go. However, finding millions of online fans and achieving stardom through the production of homemade videos are rare accomplishments—even for the most talented of groups. In fact, the vast majority of homemade music videos are clumsily produced. After their production, they are uploaded onto the Internet, where they find limited appeal on YouTube as well as other Internet sites such as WATCHitPLAYit.com and Vimeo. Many of the videos are produced simply by pointing a camera at the stage or set while the band performs; others make crude attempts to produce surreal images and dreamy sequences. Finding themselves crowded onto these sites with tens of thousands of other homemade videos, these amateur performers can only hope that lightning will strike.

Breaking Copyright Laws

Sometimes, though, lightning has been known to strike thanks to the efforts of others. It is not uncommon for fans to create music videos on their own, helping little-known bands gain traction. In 2004 Gary Brolsma, a nineteen-year-old fan of the group O-Zone, made his own video of the band's peppy dance song "Dragostea," then uploaded the video onto a number of music fan websites. The CD featuring "Dragostea" had been suffering at the bottom of the charts, but Brolsma's homemade video sparked interest in the song and sales zoomed. "The video is giving the song a second life here,"[52] said Ron Slomowicz, a DJ at a dance club in Nashville, Tennessee.

However, other fan-produced videos are not always welcome. Fans may enjoy using their home computers to splice together footage they find on the web, or even use their

Musicians Lars Ulrich and Roger McGuinn, and the chief executive officer of Napster, Hank Barry (left to right), testify before the US Senate Judiciary Committee in 2000, to share their views on music copyright and the Internet.

own cameras to shoot original scenes, but when they use recorded music and upload it onto the Internet, in many cases they are breaking copyright laws. In other words, by airing their own videos featuring other people's music, they may be denying sales of that music to the original artists and producers of the music.

Record producers have filed lawsuits against the websites that enable amateur video makers to upload their videos. In 2010 four record labels filed lawsuits against Vimeo.com because fans had posted their own videos on the site featuring music that had been copyrighted by the labels. As of 2011 these cases had not yet been resolved—often, it takes years for lawsuits to be litigated in the courts or settled out of court. Nevertheless, legal experts expect Vimeo.com to take the position that it has "fair use" of the music—that the amateurs who uploaded the videos do not expect to make profits from their videos and, therefore, the record labels are not suffering harm. Moreover, they suggest, the labels may actually profit from these homemade efforts because the songs are receiving free promotion through the efforts of the amateur video makers. Says copyright attorney Ben

Sharing Success with Miley Cyrus

People who make their own music videos don't necessarily have to be noticed by major record labels in order to find success. YouTube maintains a program that shares advertising revenue with amateur video makers whose work earns top views on the site. One amateur who takes advantage of the program is Dave Days, a musician from Los Angeles, who by 2011 had posted more than a hundred videos featuring his music on YouTube, scoring nearly 300 million views.

Many of his videos are parodies, and some of his most popular parodies have featured cardboard cutouts of Miley Cyrus. Far from being angry with Days, Cyrus's managers saw the popularity of the parodies and arranged for the pop star to appear in the 2010 video for Days's song "My Last Song for Miley Cyrus."

"A lot of people saw the video and were disappointed she wasn't cardboard," joked Days. Within a year, the video for "My Last Song for Miley Cyrus" had garnered more than 12 million views on YouTube.

Quoted in John Timpane. "Web Video Success Stories." *Philadelphia Inquirer,* October 2, 2011, p. A8.

Sheffner, "Copyright reform activists argue that they're examples of fair use tolerated under copyright law."[53]

Nevertheless, the record labels argue that posting videos online using copyrighted material is a form of illegal file sharing—an issue that has already been decided in the courts. In 2001 the music file-sharing site Napster was sued by rap star Dr. Dre and metal band Metallica member Lars Ulrich as well as their labels, who contended that they were being denied royalties because fans had access to their music for free on the site. Napster settled the suits by paying millions of dollars in damages to the artists and their labels, and by agreeing to shut down as a file-sharing site. (Napster has since been restarted as a legal music sales site.) Although Napster no longer enables fans to share music for free, it is still widely believed that illegal file sharing on the web remains rampant.

Crossing the Threshold

While the courts sort through the legal issues involved with the production of homemade music videos, there is no question that bands will continue to use their talents and limited resources to produce their own music videos. Certainly, the videos they churn out will lack the production values of videos produced for big-time stars like Lady Gaga and Beyoncé. Such videos take hundreds of thousands, if not millions, of dollars to produce. In addition to top-tier directors, the crews for professional music videos include set designers, costume designers, choreographers, dancers, makeup artists, sound technicians, camera operators, lighting specialists, writers to sketch out the scenarios, and numerous other professionals. Moreover, expensive sets are often built specifically for the video productions, usually utilizing professional studios and soundstages. And the equipment used to produce the videos is far superior than the inexpensive gear available to consumers. Finally, the record labels typically provide big budgets to promote the videos prior to their premieres.

Nevertheless, artists like Devo, Soulja Boy, and OK Go managed to break through the enormous barriers that stood in their way. They were able to produce inexpensive videos on their own that helped lead them into successful music careers. As music videos move forward, it is likely that other talented performers will find that making their own videos will also help them cross the threshold into stardom.

CHAPTER 6

The Future of Music Videos

Fans of John Mayer can do more than watch the singer's music videos. They can appear in them, too.

Mayer is among a growing group of pop stars to add an interactive feature to their videos. To participate, fans need webcams and must download an app from Mayer's website. By using the app and transmitting their own images through their webcams, fans can place themselves in the background as the video plays on their computer screens. Mayer first invited fans to use the app in 2009 when he released his album *Battle Studies*. To help promote the CD, Mayer produced a video for the song "Heartbreak Warfare" that features the interactive application. "We found a real positive reaction to it," says Kristin Zovich, a marketing executive who helped promote the video. "It's just a different way to deliver content to fans so it's not just 'click here and go to YouTube.' It's a little bit more creative."[54]

The ability of fans to interact with Mayer's videos illustrates that as the production of music videos moves further into the twenty-first century, artists, producers, and other creative people have concluded that they must offer something more to fans than simply a three- or four-minute clip featuring music, dancing, and surreal special effects. It is clear that in the future music videos will become even more interactive—employing the Internet and an assortment of new apps that will provide fans opportunities to participate in the videos. "I don't think by any means this will be a flash in the pan," says Zovich. "This will be something that will become more commonplace."[55]

Augmented Reality

Other performers have taken the concept of interaction a step further. For example, in 2009 reggae-pop singer Sean Kingston made an app available to his fans that allows them to download a video in which an animated version of the singer, known as Li'l Sean, performs alongside his fans, who add footage of themselves singing and dancing to his single "Fire Burning." "It's all about the one-to-one marketing that we as labels tend to lose," says Lee Stimmel, vice president of marketing for Epic Records, Kingston's label. "If I got a 10-year-old kid to get engaged with Sean Kingston by

Sean Kingston arrives with his animated alter ego, Li'l Sean, at the 2009 MTV Video Music Awards.

building a video and showing it to his buddies, I just turned on four more guys and gals to him. That has to resonate with entertainment going forward."[56]

The same year that Kingston released "Fire Burning," the Australian rock band Lost Valentinos made a similar app available to their fans in which the fans could pick out their favorite members of the band, then place the video images of the band members in backgrounds they filmed on their own. Fans responded with some truly innovative creations, inserting the band members onto their shoulders, displaying them on their desktops, slipping through bathroom sinks, and rocking on oceanfront piers.

The technique is known as augmented reality, or the interaction between the live world and images that are computer-generated. Sports fans have been watching examples of augmented reality for years. When TV networks broadcast professional and college football games, video technicians are able to add yellow lines showing the yard line the offense must reach in order to make a first down. As seen on TV, the yellow line seems real—the players appear to cross over the line. Hockey fans have also seen examples of augmented reality when TV broadcasters add a streak behind the puck, which helps fans at home locate the direction of the small black disk in what can be a very fast-moving game.

Changing the Music, Too

The efforts by performers like Sean Kingston and the Lost Valentinos give fans the tools they need to add their own images to the videos. In 2011 Icelandic pop star Björk offered a similar interactive feature for fans of her album *Biophilia*, enabling them to take her videos and add visual enhancements provided through her website. In other words, fans can serve as post-production technicians, adding the special effects they prefer to see in her videos.

Björk's ten-track album was released as a CD as well as an MP3 file. The interactive feature is available to the fans who choose the MP3 format, enabling them to download the music as well as a suite of applications that make it

possible for them to interact with the files. For example, one of the songs on the album is "Virus," which tells the story of a deadly parasitic infection. In the video, fans can help Björk fight off the infection by sending healthy purple cells to battle the green parasitic cells. In the video for the song "Crystalline," fans can add animated crystals of varying colors as the song's story takes them through a dark tunnel. "I didn't want the connection between the song and the app to be superficial," says Björk. "It had to go to the core."[57]

In fact, Björk took the process even a step further by including an app that enables her fans to change the music—a feature that would probably make many professional singers and musicians blanch at the thought that their work could be altered by their fans. But Björk believes that to truly connect with her fans, they should have the tools to add their own musical touches to the videos. "Her audience has come to expect the unexpected from her,"[58] says Peter Clancy, vice president of Nonesuch Records, Björk's label.

Breaking Down the Barriers

Although Björk and other performers provide their fans with tools to alter their videos, the videos for the music world's brightest stars are still made by professionals—top directors, choreographers, and others whose talents are very much in demand. In fact, many of Hollywood's top directors got their start by directing music videos—among them are Spike Jonze, director of *Where the Wild Things Are*; David Fincher, director of *The Social Network*; Michel Gondrey, who directed *The Green Hornet*; and Michael Bay, who has directed the films in the *Transformers* series.

These and others directors are known for their high-quality work, but does an adult director well into his thirties, forties, or beyond truly know what may appeal to a teenage music fan? Some record company executives have conceded that their young fans may know more about what they like in a music video than the adult professionals who

Björk performs one of her visually elaborate shows at Westergaspark in the Netherlands in 2007.

The First Interactive Video

What may have been the first interactive video was produced in 2003 for the British band Hell is for Heroes. The Internet-based video was made for the band's song "You Drove Me To It." The video included a character dressed entirely in red. When the red-clad figure appeared on screen, it served as a signal to fans to open links on the band's website. The password needed to open the links was provided every time the red-clad figure appeared in the video.

When fans followed the links, they found new photos of band members, dates for the band's tours, and other news about the band. Eric Wimbolt, head of new media for EMI, the band's label, said young fans appreciate bands that take risks with new technology. He says, "It positions a band very well if they're seen to be embracing new technology—to be seen to be risk-taking and innovative creatively."

Quoted in Owen Gibson. "Red or Dead." *Guardian*, May 12, 2003, p. C48.

are paid to write, direct, design, and choreograph the videos. That is why some labels have experimented with incorporating fan-provided footage and other materials into the videos of their performers. Ross Martin, the vice president of programming for mtvU says, "The music video process is another way of tearing down the wall between bands and fans."[59]

When the pop singer Francesca Battistelli released her single "This Is the Stuff" in 2011, she filmed a professionally produced video featuring the singer lamenting about stumbling through the hurdles of everyday life. The video features Battistelli living in a surreal world of cardboard houses and cars. But the singer also released a second video for the song, composed entirely of footage of her concerts and rehearsals that had been shot by fans. Battistelli even invited some fans to bring their cameras right onto the stage so they could shoot close-ups of the singer and her backup musicians. Later, the footage submitted by several of her fans was spliced together into a three-minute video. "I have the best fans and feel so blessed," says Battistelli. "It was so fun to have them be my directors and stand right up on the stage with me every night."[60]

The Vaccines, a British rock group, made a similar video when the band invited its fans to provide still photographs to be used in the video for the band's song "Wetsuit." As a result, the video is composed almost entirely of hundreds of photos sent by fans. In fact, the video director had to cull through some three thousand photos before picking the shots used to illustrate the video. "We always talk about breaking down the barriers between the band and the fans," says Vaccines singer Justin Young. "We like sharing music with them, meeting them, interacting with them, as most bands do. So this felt like the ultimate interaction."[61]

A Music Video Around the Corner

If fans don't want to offer their own still photos or digital footage to their favorite performers, there are other ways for them to interact with the videos. Google, the Mountain View, California, company that produces the world's most popular search engine, has found a way to make music videos interactive by employing its Google Maps feature.

The first group to incorporate Google Maps into a music video was the Canadian rock band Arcade Fire, which in 2010 released a video for its song "The Wilderness Downtown" on the Internet. When a fan watching the video keys in his or her home address, the video opens a link to Google Maps, which then provides a view of the fan's neighborhood. Therefore, the fan can create a music video of Arcade Fire performing "The Wilderness Downtown" just down the street from the fan's house, or perhaps in front of the local high school, or other places in the fan's neighborhood. Says music historian Alan Cross, "When you see

Francesca Battistelli, seen here performing in Nashville in 2009, released a video in 2011 composed entirely of snippets of video footage submitted by fans.

something like that, it's an example of 'Wow, I guess everything hasn't been done yet.'"[62]

Google also helped in the production of the video for the 2011 song "3 Dreams of Black." As the video begins, the viewer sees three virtual worlds displayed on the screen. Fans can follow the video as it moves through the three worlds. The video is also interactive—fans can use their computers to pan from side to side so they can see action that is occurring off-camera. At the end of the video, fans can create their own animated characters and embed them into the video.

Video Game Action

If the scenario for *3 Dreams of Black* seems as though it emerged from a video game, well, that was the intention all along. Thanks to the enormous popularity of video games, music video producers believe they can lure gaming fans to the videos if the videos are made to look like games.

The director of the *3 Dreams of Black* video is Chris Milk, a veteran director who has worked with Kanye West, Green Day, Gnarls Barkley, and Arcade Fire, among others. To produce the video, Milk enlisted the aid of Aaron Koblin, head of Google's Creative Lab Data Arts Team. In making the video, Milk and Koblin employed technology known as Web-Based Graphics Library, or WebGL. It is the same technology used in most video games that enables the players to create characters, fire weapons, or have their characters leap through exploding debris and other mayhem. "WebGL essentially transforms your browser into an open-source video game console,"[63] says Thomas Gayno, marketing manager for Google Creative Lab. And so while the fan is negotiating through the surreal world created for them through the WebGL process, singer Norah Jones adds the vocals for "3 Dreams of Black," the song played during the video.

"We both see technology as a means to tell human stories," says Milk. "[Computer] code is a canvas, just like cinema or television."[64] Adds Koblin, "I've honestly never thought of it as music marketing. It's a magical transforma-

Videos in 3-D

As music videos move into the future, fans may find it necessary to keep their 3-D glasses close at hand. As the technology for 3-D television improves, it is anticipated that more programming will be available for home viewing in 3-D—including music videos. Rapper Missy Elliott is believed to be the first artist to produce 3-D videos for her 2008 songs "Shake Your Pom Pom" and "Ching-A-Ling," both from her *Step Up 2 the Streets* CD.

"This is truly historic," said Dave Meyers, who has provided special effects for several of Elliott's videos. "People have talked about and tried to make it happen before, but no one has ever set out to purposefully create a 3D music video and then actually made it happen."

Quoted in Artist Direct. "Missy Elliott Makes First 3D Music Video." January 31, 2008. www.artistdirect.com/nad/news/article/0,,4559263,00.html.

Missy Elliott wears 3-D glasses to a taping of MTV's Total Request Live *to promote her 2008 videos that use 3-D technology.*

tion that leads you into a different space and blesses you with a new perspective."[65]

Product Placement

There is no question that the videos made by Björk, Sean Kingston, Francesca Battistelli, Arcade Fire, and the other performers help those artists form bonds with their fans. Record company executives firmly believe that with numerous forms of entertainment available to young people—TV, movies, video games, and surfing the Internet—the only way music videos can survive as a marketable form of entertainment is for the performers to do more to interact with their fans.

Record companies believe the artists can help build something close to a personal relationship with their fans if the fans become part of the process to produce the video—even if the fans' photos or digital footage are ultimately not used. "It's hard to [bring out] a record these days—it takes a lot more avenues of exposure," says Lee Stimmel. "We always push to the fans."[66]

Snacking on Music Videos

If apparel companies or snack food makers can place their products in music videos, is it also possible for consumers to find music videos stuffed inside bags of potato chips? The answer is no—but buying certain consumer products can give consumers access to online content, including music videos.

In 2009 the snack food company Frito-Lay marketed bags of Doritos tortilla chips that featured special logos on the bags. Fans who held the logos up to their webcams while visiting the Doritos website could launch videos by the artists Big Boi or Blink-182. Moreover, the videos were interactive: By changing the position of the bag, fans could see the videos from different angles. There was even a feature that enabled fans to add their own backgrounds to the scene. And the videos were shot in 3-D. "An online 3D performance was something we just had to be part of," said Blink-182 vocalist and bassist Mark Hoppus. "As big technology guys, we're pumped that people can now experience a little bit of our summer tour through something as accessible as a bag of Doritos and a computer."

Quoted in Lewis Wallace. "Blink-182 Rocks 'Augmented Reality' Show in Doritos Bag." *Wired*, July 6, 2009. www.wired.com/underwire/2009/07/blink-182-rocks-augmented-reality-show-in-doritos-bag.

In fact, getting fans to feel a personal involvement in the video has benefits other than simply helping sell albums. One of the newest trends in music video production is to use the video to sell products to the people watching at home. This so-called product placement strategy has been in use in movie and TV production for years. Manufacturers of dish detergent, potato chips, automobiles, pet food, and hundreds of other consumer goods have been willing to pay fees to studios and networks so that their products will be placed in the scenes and visible to the audience.

For fans who watch music videos on their computer screens, the producers have taken product placement a step further. Under the concept, if a fan is watching the video of a favorite band and wants to know where to buy the shirt worn by the drummer, the fan can mouse over the image of the drummer on the screen and a pop-up box will appear, providing information on the price as well as the retailers where the shirt is available. The first video to feature this marketing tool was produced for Irish rock band The Script for the group's 2008 song "Breakeven." According

Irish rock band The Script, seen here performing at the O2 Arena in London, England, had the first video with an interactive product placement feature.

to the video's producers, there are 242 products advertised in the video. "Attaching [marketing content] to music videos seems like a smart idea," says Paul Verna, an Internet marketing analyst, "given . . . how amenable the viewing audience seems to be to receiving advertising messages."[67] Other recording stars who have made their videos available for product marketing are Lady Gaga, Jonas Brothers, and Miley Cyrus.

However, not all fans are happy about the trend toward making music videos into marketing tools. Says Sarah Murphy, a Massachusetts college student, "Music videos are a way for artists to express themselves visually, giving fans a new glimpse at their idols and heroes. Music videos should leave you in awe, questioning what just happened, looking for answers and discussing the content with friends. . . . Music videos are themselves an advertisement for the artists and should not be ruined by a blatant attempt to promote Coke or McDonald's."[68]

Keeping Fans in Awe

Although product placement in music videos may have its critics, the financial incentives companies offer to musicians and their producers have helped widen the audiences for the videos, often creating a worldwide stage for the performers. When MTV was first getting underway, the only viewers who could see the new network's programming were the residents of New Jersey who were wired for cable. Now, when a band posts its video online, it could potentially reach an audience that may number in the billions. Moreover, with the development of smartphones and tablets, fans can access music videos through the Internet and watch them whenever and wherever they please. Indeed, the viewership for many music videos found on the Internet is astronomical. By 2010, Lady Gaga's video for "Bad Romance" had been viewed nearly 250 million times on YouTube. The video for Justin Bieber's song "Baby" had been viewed about 243 million times on YouTube. Miley Cyrus's video for her song "Party in the USA" was watched 138 million times by her fans.

There is no question that the Internet as well as the new interactive features of the videos have helped spark new life into music videos. In recent years broadcast TV has been able to draw huge audiences for shows like *American Idol*, *The Voice*, *The X Factor*, and *The Sing-Off*. These shows are now providing the prime-time platform for music on TV, meaning music videos have been mostly pushed to smaller cable outlets. Even MTV has made the switch, finding that its most popular shows are reality-based, such as *America's Best Dance Crew* and *Jersey Shore*. Says music critic Ramin Setoodeh, "The reason music videos have come back from the dead is simple. They are the perfect length—three to five minutes—for abbreviated online attention spans. They are easy to share, tweet, Facebook and comment on. You can watch them from the comfort of your own home (or cubicle, when you're procrastinating at work)."[69]

Indeed, music videos have come a long way since they were first produced in the 1970s. Most videos are just as surreal as ever, but the computer-generated special effects, production values, and the drive to make videos interactive have taken them to visual heights unforeseen in the days when images of Mike Nesmith and his backup singers were superimposed over ocean waves, or when the camera filmed Queen performing "Bohemian Rhapsody" mostly in shadows.

During the 1980s, artists like Michael Jackson and Madonna set the bar high for the level of performance that could be achieved in the very short time span found in the typical music video. In subsequent years, other performers have met that challenge, and now truly incandescent performances can be found in the videos produced for Lady Gaga, Taylor Swift, Beyoncé, Britney Spears, and other stars. There is no question that, in the future, music videos will continue to awe fans while setting even higher standards for the performers and the technical experts whose talents will be tested by one of popular culture's most dazzling forms of art.

NOTES

Introduction: The Emotional Power of Music Videos

1. Quoted in Daniel Kreps. "Kanye West Storms the VMA Stage During Taylor Swift's Speech." *Rolling Stone*, September 13, 2009. www.rollingstone.com/music/news/kanye-west-storms-the-vmas-stage-during-taylor-swifts-speech-20090913.
2. Quoted in Kreps. "Kanye West Storms the VMA Stage."
3. Quoted in Steve Pond. "The Industry in the Eighties." *Rolling Stone*, November 15, 1990, p. 113+.

Chapter 1: The Roots of Music on Video

4. Nathan Miller. *New World Coming: The 1920s and the Making of Modern America*. Cambridge, MA.: De Capo Press, 2003, p. 339.
5. Quoted in Donald Crafton. *The Talkies: American Cinema's Transition to Sound, 1926–1931*. Berkeley: University of California Press, 1999, p. 109.
6. Quoted in Christopher Feldman. *The Billboard Book of Number Two Singles*. New York: Billboard

Books, 2000, p. 195.
7. Jim Farber and Glenn Kenny. "The Top 100 Music Videos." *Rolling Stone*, October 14, 1992, p. 65+.
8. Saul Austerlitz. *Money for Nothing: A History of the Music Video from the Beatles to the White Stripes*. New York: Continuum, 2007, pp. 17–18.
9. Austerlitz. *Money for Nothing*, p. 19.
10. Quoted in Yardena Arar. "Ex-Monkee Swings Over to Videodiscs." *Chicago Tribune*, October 25, 1991, p. E25.

Chapter 2: "I Want My MTV"

11. Quoted in History.com. "MTV Launches," 2011. www.history.com/this-day-in-history/mtv-launches.
12. Quoted in Greg Prato. *MTV Ruled the World: The Early Years of Music Video*. London: Lulu, 2010, p. 97.
13. Quoted in Prato. *MTV Ruled the World*, pp. 32–33.
14. Quoted in Sheila Marikar. "MTV at 30: Original Veejays, Where Are They Now?" ABC News, August 1, 2011. http://abcnews.go.com/Entertainment

/mtvs-original-veejays-now/story?id=14204034#2.

15. Quoted in Prato. *MTV Ruled the World*, p. 90.

16. Lisa D. Campbell. *Michael Jackson: The King of Pop*. Boston: Branden, 1993, p. 58.

17. Campbell. *Michael Jackson*, p. 60.

18. Quoted in Farber and Kenny. "The Top 100 Music Videos," p. 65.

19. Quoted in Farber and Kenny. "The Top 100 Music Videos," p. 65.

20. Quoted in *New York Times*. "Tipper Gore Widens War on Rock." January 4, 1988, p. C18.

21. Quoted in *New York Times*. "Tipper Gore Widens War on Rock," p. C18.

Chapter 3: The Art of Music Videos

22. Quoted in Rob Markman. "Mac Miller Breaks Down 'Frick Park Market.'" September 30, 2011. www.mtv.com/news/articles/1671779/mac-miller-frick-park-market-video.jhtml.

23. Quoted in René Passeron. *Surrealism*. Paris: Terrail, 2001, p. 44.

24. Passeron. *Surrealism*, p. 82.

25. Cynthia Marie Erb. *Tracking King Kong: A Hollywood Icon in World Culture*. Detroit: Wayne State University Press, 2009, p. 110.

26. Carol Vernallis. "Strange People, Weird Objects: The Nature of Narrative, Character, and Editing in Music Videos." In *Medium Cool: Music Videos from Soundies to Cellphones*, edited by Roger Beebe and Jason Middleton. Durham, N.C.: Duke University Press, 2007, p. 113.

27. Amy Schriefer. "The Decade in Music: Britney Spears' 'Toxic.'" National Public Radio, November 13, 2009. www.npr.org/templates/story/story.php?storyId=120385043.

28. James Montgomery. "Katy Perry's 'California Gurls' Video: So Sweet It Hurts." June 15, 2010. www.mtv.com/news/articles/1641591/katy-perrys-california-gurls-video-so-sweet-it-hurts.jhtml.

Chapter 4: When Music Videos Make Political and Social Statements

29. Austerlitz, *Money for Nothing*, p. 49.

30. Quoted in Georgia Dullea. "Madonna's New Beat Is a Hit, But Song's Message Rankles." *New York Times*, September 18, 1986, p. B1.

31. Quoted in Dullea, "Madonna's New Beat Is a Hit," p. B1.

32. Ellen Goodman. "No Sermon, Madonna, If You Cut the Propaganda." *Los Angeles Times*, September 23, 1986, p. B5.

33. Quoted in Rikky Rooksby. *Madonna: The Complete Guide to Her Music*. London: Omnibus Press, 2004, p. 21.

34. Denise Sullivan. *Keep on Pushing: Black Power Music from Blues to Hip-Hop*. Chicago: Lawrence Hill, 2011, p. 206.

35. Quoted in Chris Willman. "Coolio." *Entertainment Weekly*, December 29, 1995, p. 46+.

36. Quoted in Courtney Crowder. "Lady Gaga's New Video Explained: Dead Diners, Americana and Cigarette Sunglasses." ABC News, March 16, 2010. http://abcnews.go.com/Entertainment/SpringConcert/decoding-lady-gagas-telephone-video/story?id=10114081.

37. Quoted in Crowder. "Lady Gaga's New Video Explained."

38. Quoted in Crowder. "Lady Gaga's New Video Explained."

39. Quoted in Crowder. "Lady Gaga's New Video Explained."

40. Quoted in Crowder. "Lady Gaga's New Video Explained."

41. Quoted in Justin Matthews. "Fox News Contributor Calls Lady Gaga's 'Telephone' Video Poison." Musictoob, March 19, 2010. http://new.music.yahoo.com/blogs/musictoob/29181/fox-news-contributor-calls-lady-gagas-telephone-video-poison.

42. Armond White. "Going Gaga: Thank Tarantino for the Berserk Feminism in *Kick-Ass* and in Lady Gaga's 'Telephone.'" *New York Press*, April 16, 2010. www.nypress.com/article-21128-going-gaga.html.

Chapter 5: Making Music Videos at Home

43. Richard Cromelin. "Pop, Rock, Blues by Mink DeVille and Devo at Santa Monica Civic." *Los Angeles Times*, January 3, 1978, p. E7.

44. Quoted in Richard Cromelin. "Spud Report: Devo Does Its Duty." *Los Angeles Times*, July 1, 1979, p. M71.

45. Quoted in Greg Jarboe. *YouTube and Video Marketing: An Hour a Day*. Indianapolis: Wiley, 2012, p. 111.

46. Quoted in Moira McCormick. "Videotapes Help Chicago Bands to Promote Disks, Themselves." *Billboard*, August 29, 1981, p. 32.

47. Quoted in McCormick. "Videotapes Help Chicago Bands," p. 32.

48. Quoted in J.G. Harding. "Adam Powell: How I Became a Music Video Director." *Sound on Sound*, February 2011. www.soundonsound.com/sos/feb11/articles/adam-powell.htm.

49. Quoted in Mariel Concepcion. "YouTube." *Billboard*, September 27, 2008, p. 17+.

50. Quoted in Concepcion. "YouTube," p. 17+.

51. Quoted in Brittney Moody. "Area Band Produces First Music Video." Farmington Hills Patch, January 30, 2011. http://farmington-mi.patch.com/articles/area-band-produces-first-music-video-3.

52. Quoted in Michael Paoletta. "Web Clip Buoys Novelty Song." *Billboard*, March 19, 2005, p. 28.

53. Ben Sheffner. "Money Clip." *Billboard*, January 23, 2010, p. 17.

Chapter 6: The Future of Music Videos

54. Quoted in Antony Bruno. "Reality Bytes." *Billboard*, November 28, 2009, p. 8.
55. Quoted in Bruno. "Reality Bytes," p. 8.
56. Quoted in *Billboard*. "The Technology of Tomorrow." August 29, 2009, p. 26.
57. Quoted in *Billboard*. "It's In Our Hands." July 30, 2011, p. 20+.
58. Quoted in *Billboard*. "It's In Our Hands," p. 20+.
59. Quoted in Cortney Harding. "Video To Go." *Billboard*, November 29, 2008, p. 9.
60. Quoted in Urban Christian News. "'This Is the Stuff': Francesca Battistelli Unveils Fan Directed Music Video for No. 1 Hit Song." May 4, 2011. www.urbanchristiannews .com/ucn/2011/05/this-is-the -stuff-francesca-battistelli-un veils-fan-directed-music-video -for-1-hit-song.html.
61. Quoted in Huffington Post. "Band Releases First Music Video Made Using Instagram." October 13, 2011. www.huffingtonpost .com/2011/10/13/watch-band -releases-first_n_1008773.html.
62. Quoted in Angelina Chapin. "Google Resurrects the Video Star." *Canadian Business*, October 11, 2010, p. 81.
63. Quoted in John Pavlus. "Are Videogames the Future of Music Videos?" Fast Company Design, May 16, 2011. www.fastcodesign .com/1663841/are-videogames -the-future-of-music-videos -chris-milk-and-google-create-3 -d-world.
64. Quoted in Ann-Christine Diaz. "The Creativity 50." *Advertising Age*, June 6, 2011, p. 8.
65. Quoted in Diaz, "The Creativity 50," p. 8.
66. Quoted in Brian Hiatt. "How to Sell a Smash Hit." *Rolling Stone*, September 7, 2006, p. 19+.
67. Quoted in Evie Nagy. "Click This." *Billboard*, January 31, 2009, p. 8.
68. Sarah Murphy. "The Future of Music Videos?" *Mount Holyoke News*, May 19, 2010. http://themhnews .org/2010/05/blogs/rewind/the -future-of-music-videos.
69. Ramin Setoodeh. "I Want My Music Videos!" *Newsweek*, July 26, 2010, p. 52+.

Films

The Beatles

A Hard Day's Night, 1964

The Beatles spend one madcap day preparing for a concert. Each musical performance is filmed as though it could be a stand-alone music video, with the four lads frolicking through the city as their music plays in the background.

Walt Disney

Fantasia, 1940

This animated film features a series of unconnected vignettes set to classical music. The off-the-wall scenarios—such as the scene in which hippos dance with crocodiles—would later inspire music video directors to let their imaginations run wild.

Al Jolson

The Jazz Singer, 1927

This story of a singer's rise to stardom and his strained relationship with his father is the first film in which audio is synchronized to the moving images on screen. Early in the film Jolson sings "Toot, Toot, Tootsie," marking the first time a song is performed on film.

Marilyn Monroe

Gentlemen Prefer Blondes, 1953

Madonna's admiration for the scene in which Monroe performs "Diamonds Are a Girl's Best Friend" inspired the pop star to copy it for the 1985 video for her song "Material Girl."

Elvis Presley

Jailhouse Rock, 1957

The story tells the dour tale of a young man sent to prison for killing a man in a bar fight. By the end of the movie, Presley's character has emerged as a rock-and-roll star; his performance of the title song can stand alone as a music video, as everybody—guards and prisoners alike—rock along with the star.

Music Videos

Francesca Battistelli

This Is the Stuff, 2011

Battistelli released two videos for the single: one produced by professionals, the other made by fans who were often invited onstage to film close-ups of the singer and her band. Her effort illustrates a new trend in music video production of letting the fans help make the video.

The Buggles

Video Killed the Radio Star, 1979

The video presents a surreal world in which a little girl wanders through a mishmash of TV sets and radios. The video was the first video broadcast on MTV in 1981. The Buggles were never able to capitalize on their brief moment in history; by the time the video aired, the band had already broken up.

Coolio

Gangsta's Paradise, 1995

The hip-hop star uses the haunting and pulsating rhythms of the song and video to paint a bleak picture of ghetto life—one dominated by drugs and gun violence.

Missy Elliott

Ching-A-Ling and Shake Your Pom Pom, 2008

The two videos made for Elliott's songs marked a milestone in music video production because they were the first ones filmed in 3-D.

Peter Gabriel

Sledgehammer, 1986

Rolling Stone has declared the video for "Sledgehammer" among the best videos ever filmed. It took a week to film the five-minute video, in which Gabriel's face is re-created in vegetables, surrounded by a train, hounded by puppets, and forced to watch a cabaret show starring headless chickens.

Michael Jackson

Beat It, Billie Jean, and Thriller, 1983

These three videos set the gold standard for music video quality thanks to the special effects, camera work, and sheer talent of the performer. The tight choreography for *Thriller* can still be seen—mostly at high school proms.

Lady Gaga and Beyoncé

Telephone, 2010

The two singers made a lot of statements in this video, commenting on the ill treatment of women in prison, the personal prisons women face as they search for their own identities, and how women have the power to rise up in rebellion against the lifestyles dictated for them.

Joi Lansing

Trapped in the Web of Love, 1966

Produced for Scopitone machines, Lansing's video portrayed the singer pining away for her lost love while tangled in a giant spider web—the type of strange and unreal scenario that music video producers would later embrace.

Cyndi Lauper

Girls Just Wanna Have Fun, 1983

One of the first videos to make a social statement, this video provides a message of female empowerment. Lauper tells her fans that youth is too important a time to waste and girls should not be that concerned with the approval of their parents.

Madonna

Papa Don't Preach, 1986

Madonna makes a statement calling for the empowerment of women to make their own decisions. Since the decision in the video concerns having a baby out of wedlock, the video sparked a national argument between pro-choice advocates and activists who oppose abortion rights.

John Mayer

Heartbreak Warfare, 2009

In one of the first attempts to create an interactive video, fans could submit webcam images of themselves to Mayer's website, which were then embedded into the background of the video.

Mac Miller

Frick Park Market, 2011

Miller hands a turkey sandwich to a clone of himself, then enters a mystical world of dancing rabbits, bears, and storks. The video is a clear example of how surrealism continues to dominate the production of music videos.

Mike Nesmith

Elephant Parts, 1981

The hour-long TV pilot featured five music videos by the ex-Monkee. Nesmith failed to sell the pilot to a TV network, but the video helped convince executives at Warner Communications that a cable TV channel devoted entirely to music videos could be successful. As such, Nesmith's work served as an inspiration for the creation of MTV.

OK Go

Here It Goes Again, 2007

The little-known band made their own video, performing the song while dancing on treadmills. The video went viral on the Internet and won the Grammy Award for Best Music Video.

Katy Perry

California Gurls, 2010

The producers of this video turned California into a giant Candy Land game. The imaginative video shows Perry encountering grumpy Gummi Bears, saving her friend from a prison of bubble gum, and drowning rap star Snoop Dogg in a mountain of whipped cream.

Public Enemy

Fight the Power, 1989

Twenty-five years after the adoption of

the US Civil Rights Act, Public Enemy charged that African Americans had not yet achieved equality with white Americans. The video depicts a huge rally in which the rappers challenge blacks to stop talking and start fighting.

Queen

Bohemian Rhapsody, 1975

Believed to be the first actual music video, it was aired on the TV show *Midnight Special*. The video is mostly composed of the band members on stage, but does include some special effects such as double exposures, shadowy images, and scenes that appeared to have been filmed through a prism.

Britney Spears

Toxic, 2004

The singer put her sex appeal on display as she changed from airline flight attendant to nearly nude dancer to wronged woman capable of scaling skyscrapers in search of her unfaithful boyfriend—all within three minutes and thirty-two seconds.

Taylor Swift

You Belong with Me, 2009

The simple story of two young people finding love features no camera tricks, overt sexuality, or special effects, proving that music videos do not have to rely on surrealism to tell their stories.

30 Seconds to Mars

From Yesterday, 2005

At a cost of $13 million, *From Yesterday* is the most expensive music video ever made. To film the video, the band members traveled to China, where elaborate sets were constructed and three hundred extras were recruited and dressed in medieval-style costumes.

censorship: Power held by the government or other authority that prevents the publication of books, newspapers, or magazines because of their content. Censors can also block movies and music videos as well as TV and radio broadcasts. In America, Congress has severely limited censorship because the US Constitution guarantees freedom of expression.

copyright: Law that provides writers, artists, musicians, and other creative people protection against others who may profit from their work.

demographics: Statistical study of a population meant to determine the numerical value of age groups, gender, residency, and similar factors. TV networks often attempt to tailor their programming to specific demographics of viewers.

gangsta: The gangsta lifestyle describes a world of drugs, guns, and violence found on the streets of urban American neighborhoods. Gangsta rappers tell stories of crime and violence in their rhymes.

narrowcasting: Strategy adopted by cable TV networks to target specific audiences with programming geared to their interests.

new wave: Experimental form of music that first surfaced in the 1970s; it features loud and pulsating rhythms created by synthesizers and other electric instruments.

Orwellian society: The term is based on the 1949 novel *1984* by British author George Orwell, which tells the story of people forced to live under a totalitarian dictatorship. In an Orwellian society, few people enjoy civil liberties or privacy and are closely watched by the evil forces of the government.

pilot: Many TV shows start out as pilots, which are test episodes. Pilots are frequently aired to gauge audience enthusiasm for the shows; if the TV network perceives that the pilot has been successful, it may contract with the producers to film a season's worth of shows.

rabbit ears: In the pre-cable era, most TV sets were equipped with antennae that could be extended several feet and also rotated, enabling the viewers to achieve better reception.

Scopitone: First installed in diners, nightclubs, and taverns in the 1950s, the Scopitone machines featured a wide assortment of brief films showcasing musical acts. Performers produced films specifically for the Scopitone machines; these films often relied on scenarios similar to what could later be found in music videos.

Soundies: First installed in diners, taverns, and similar places in the 1940s, the machines served as video jukeboxes. For ten cents a viewer could watch a brief film that featured a musical act.

surrealism: Artistic movement born in 1920s Paris. Surrealists attempt to merge imaginary scenes or figures with backgrounds drawn from the real world. Surrealism has been the dominant influence on music videos from their earliest days of production.

V-chip: Device that can be installed on a television that enables parents to block programming they feel is inappropriate for their children.

veejay: Term applied to the on-air personalities during the early days of MTV. Like their counterparts on radio, the MTV veejays introduced the videos while making their personalities and commentaries part of their shows.

vinyl 45: Small records composed of stiff vinyl that played at 45 rpms (revolutions per minute) on record turntables. The 45s usually featured one song on each side.

Books

Saul Austerlitz. *Money for Nothing: A History of the Music Video from the Beatles to the White Stripes.* New York: Continuum, 2007. Austerlitz, a noted music historian and critic, provides an overview of music video history, particularly the formative years of the medium as the Beatles and the Monkees rose to stardom.

Roger Beebe and Jason Middleton, editors. *Medium Cool: Music Videos from Soundies to Cellphones.* Durham, NC: Duke University Press, 2007. Thirteen contributors, all university professors of media studies, provide their perspectives on the growth of music videos as a form of artistic expression.

Craig Marks and Rob Tannenbaum. *I Want My MTV: The Uncensored Story of the Music Video Revolution.* New York: Dutton, 2011. Although the authors concentrate on the early history of the music video network, they also take readers back to the early years of the twentieth century when cameras and audio equipment first started recording music on film.

John Mundy. *Popular Music on the Screen: From Hollywood Musical to Music Video.* Manchester, England: Manchester University Press, 1999. The author provides a thorough account of how the movie musicals of the 1930s, 1940s, and 1950s served as inspiration for future music video producers.

Greg Prato. *MTV Ruled the World: The Early Years of Music Video.* London: Lulu, 2010. Prato interviewed more than seventy musicians, producers, directors, veejays, and other professionals to chart the rise of MTV.

Periodicals

David Crook. "Ex-Monkee Nesmith: Video's New-Wave Guru." *Los Angeles Times*, April 30, 1981.

Richard Harrington. "The Spinning Image: Pop Music Goes Video." *Washington Post*, February 1, 1981.

Meg James. "3 Decades Later, MTV Wants Its Millennials." *Philadelphia Inquirer*, October 11, 2011.

David Knight, Neon Kelly, Owen Lawrence, and Sharon Steinbach. "25 Videos That Changed the World," *Music Week*, September 2006.

Ramin Setoodeh. "I Want My Music Videos!" *Newsweek*, July 26, 2010.

Internet Sources

Madeline Brand. "Rise and Fall of the Scopitone Jukebox." National Public Radio, August 9, 2006. www.npr.org/templates/story/story.php?storyId=5630027.

Courtney Crowder. "Lady Gaga's New Video Explained: Dead Diners, Americana and Cigarette Sunglasses," ABC News, March 16, 2010. http://abcnews.go.com/Entertainment/SpringConcert/decoding-lady-gagas-telephone-video/story?id=10114081.

Heather Havrilesky. "The Madonna Video You Can't See on MTV." Salon.com, April 3, 2003. www.salon.com/2003/04/03/madonna_6/.

John Pavlus. "Are Videogames the Future of Music Videos?" Fast Company Design, May 16, 2011. www.fastcodesign.com/1663841/are-videogames-the-future-of-music-videos-chris-milk-and-google-create-3-d-world.

Amy Schriefer. "The Decade in Music: Britney Spears' 'Toxic.'" National Public Radio, November 13, 2009. www.npr.org/templates/story/story.php?storyId=120385043.

Websites

Billboard magazine, "21 Under 21: Music's Hottest Minors 2011" (www.billboard.com/#/features/21-under-21-music-s-hottest-minors-2011-1005372152.story). The magazine has provided a website that lists the twenty-one top music stars under the age of twenty-one, including Miley Cyrus, Miguelito, and One Direction. Each listing includes a biography of the performer, criticism of his or her work, and a music video starring the performer.

Class Act, "Those Golden Movie Musicals" (www.classicmoviemusicals.com). Dozens of movie musicals are chronicled on this webpage. Visitors can find the stories behind the making of the musicals, as well as information on the stars and directors. The listing for *Gentlemen Prefer Blondes* features a photo of Marilyn Monroe performing "Diamonds Are a Girl's Best Friend," which later inspired the music video for Madonna's song "Material Girl."

MTV, "2011 MTV Music Video Awards" (www.mtv.com/ontv/vma/2011). Each year, MTV stages a gala awards broadcast featuring the nominees and winners of the network's Music Video Awards. The companion website for the 2011 broadcast features stories, photos, and videos by Lil Wayne, Lady Gaga, Beyoncé, and other performers. The site also features links to the companion sites for past years' MTV Music Video Awards broadcasts.

MTV, "The Original MTV VJs" (www.80svjs.com). MTV has provided this site for fans to catch up with the original MTV veejays, including Nina Blackwood, Martha Quinn, and Alan Hunter. The site also includes a video of the opening seconds of the first MTV broadcast on August 1, 1981.

PBS, "Music Video 1900 Style" (http://pbskids.org/wayback/tech1900/music/index.html). The PBS show *American Experience* provides a comprehensive history of the first attempts to merge music with images on film. The website provides two magic lantern films, including *A Bird in a Gilded Cage* and *Let's Get the Umpire's Goat*.

INDEX

E

Elephant Parts (TV program), 24–25, 31
Ellington, Duke, 14
Elliott, Missy, *89*
Ernst, Max, 42–44
ESPN, 31

F

Fabian, 19
Feminists for Life in America, 56
50 Cent, *75*
Fincher, David, 85
Finders Keepers (movie), 21
Fischinger, Oscar, 15–17
Fleetwood Mac, 25, 27
Funicello, Annette, 19

G

Gabriel, Peter, 46
Gangsta culture, 61–64
Gnarls Barkley, 88
Gondrey, Michel, 85
Goodman, Ellen, 58
Goodman, Mark, *28*, 29
Gore, Al, 36
Gore, Tipper, 36–37, *37*
Grateful Dead, 48
Green Day, 88

H

Hard Day's Night (movie), 20–21, *20*
Having a Wild Weekend (movie), 21
HBO (Home Box Office), 30
Hell Is for Heroes (band), 86
Herman's Hermits, 21
Hip-hop, 7, 40, 51, 58–64
Holl, Matthias, 15
Holliday, Billie, 14
Homemade videos, 68–80

Hoppus, Mark, 90
Horn, Trevor, 38, *38*
Hunter, Alan, 27–29, *28*

I

Infinity Hour, 75, 77
Internet
    homemade videos and, 70–75
    interactive videos and, 81, 86–87
    music video platform, 39
    product placement and, 90
    See also YouTube

J

J. Geils Band, 36
Jackson, J.J., *28*, 29
Jackson, Michael, 8, 30, 32, *33*, 34, 93
John, Elton, 25
Jolson, Al, 10–12, *11*
Jonas Brothers, 92
Jones, Davy, 22
Jones, Norah, 88
Jonze, Spike, 85

K

King Kong (movie), 44–45, *45*
King, Martin Luther Jr., 59
Kingston, Sean, 82–83, *82*, 89

L

Lady Gaga, 64–67, *65*, 80, 92, 93
Landis, John, 34
Lansing, Joi, 18
László, Alexander, 15
Lauper, Cyndi, 54–55, *55*, 64, 67
Led Zeppelin, 29
Lee, Spike, 59, *61*
Li'l Sean, 82, *82*
Lost Valentinos, 83

PICTURE CREDITS

ABOUT THE AUTHOR

Hal Marcovitz is a former newspaper reporter and columnist. He has written more than 150 books for young readers. He makes his home in Chalfont, Pennsylvania.

DATE DUE

OCT 2 7 2014			